WEST COAST STORY

CHARTWELL
BOOKS INC.

in association with Phoebus

**Produced by Rob Burt
& Patsy North**

**Published by Chartwell Books Inc
A Division of Book Sales Inc
110 Enterprise Avenue
Secaucus, New Jersey 07094**

Library of Congress Catalog Card Number 77 79007

This edition © 1977
Phoebus Publishing Company
BPC Publishing Limited
169 Wardour Street
London W1A 2JX
This material first appeared in
The Story of Pop © 1973/74/75
BPC Publishing Limited

ISBN 0 89009 141 2

Made and printed in England by Waterlow
(Dunstable) Limited

WEST COAST STORY

Music explodes out of the West Coast!
Since the early '60s— and well before the
Beatles burst from Liverpool— California
has been the centre for all that's best in
rock. This is the story of the stars, groups,
cults and trends that have emerged from
two cities teeming with talent— Los
Angeles and San Francisco.

The book is divided into three parts, each
describing the growth of West Coast music
with picture-packed biographies of the
superstars who created it.

CONTENTS

ALL SUMMER LONG

The first great musical trend evolved from the surf, sun, sand and sport of California. Surfing provided the West Coast's young with a lifestyle, the Beach Boys put it all to music and started a craze that went around the world.

SURF/HOT ROD MUSIC

Southern California in the early '60s — long before love-ins, freakouts, flower power, race riots and psychedelia — had a gracious lifestyle. The entertainment capital of the world, famous for its movie stars, Disneyland, freeways and summer resort weather 12 months of the year.

The young Californian's life was one of simplicity, fast cars, girls, coke and beach parties. The teen idols of the era were Troy Donohue and Ed Byrnes. Troy Donohue, who first graced the screen as a beefy in bathers, romancing Sandra Dee on the beach in the film *A Summer Place*, went on to make less memorable films such as *Parrish* and *Susan Slade*, but also made a fairly successful TV series called *Surfside Six*. Another TV series, *77 Sunset Strip* produced Ed Byrnes as Kookie, the hot-rodding parkin' lot attendant folk hero of modern mobilised California, who also sang about his famous comb with Connie Stevens. Both Byrnes and Donohue epitomised the West Coast youth culture with their love of the beach and fast cars.

Surfing, the sport of Hawaiian kings, had been a popular recreation along the West Coast for some years, and had by the early '60s erupted into a whole new way of life. Taking over from the older sportsmen, an enthusiastic group of young people bound together by the surf, set themselves apart. The 'surfer' was not only different in the way he mastered his board at Malibu, but by the way he dressed. He wore *pendletons, white levis, baggies;* his hair was sun-bleached (or helped a little by peroxide), and he used slang surfing terms: 'woodie' described his souped-up old wooden-sided station wagon, which he used to haul his boards; a 'goofy foot' was a surfer who rode with his right foot forward on the board. He would most likely have a 'hobie' surfboard, built of Clark Foam, and would use a special wax to prevent him from having a 'wipe-out'. Schools were divided into the 'Surfers' and the 'Ho-Dads', who kept up a friendly rivalry.

The surfing cult also had its own publication: John Severson's *Surfer Magazine* at Dana Point, and very good surfing documentaries were being produced by Bruce Brown, an early-comer to surfing, whose first full-length surf film was *Slippery When Wet.* Released in 1959, it attracted interest among a small number of Californian teenagers. His attraction increased, however, in 1961, with *Barefoot Adventure,* and he later achieved international acclaim with *The Endless Summer* — the mythological search for a wave that used up over nine miles of film on a surfing safari around the world.

The youth of California were united by their affluence, the sunshine, and their addiction to the casual life. Their love of the physical sport of riding a wave was matched, somehow, by an aesthetic if not to say spiritual thrill of being carried by the forces of nature. Perhaps it is this that joined the surfers in a bond more firm than the usual bond between fellow sportsmen. They shared a thrill, and talked about the experience rather than simply the technique. Perhaps it was this spiritual bond that accounted for the difference between this group and others — that brought about a folklore, and a music . . .

Guitarist Dick Dale with help from his group the Del-Tones gained a reputation in the Southern California area as the 'Pied Piper of Balboa', playing weekend dances at the Rendezvous Ballroom. He introduced surf music — a gutsy instrumental sound of wailing saxes and atmospheric guitar set to a pounding twelve bar bass beat. Dale once explained how the music came about. "There was a tremendous amount of power that I felt while surfing and that feeling of power was simply transferred from myself into my guitar when I was playing surf music. I couldn't get that feeling singing, so the music took on an instrumental form." It took another group, the Beach Boys — Brian, Carl and Dennis Wilson, Mike Love and David Marks — to add a lyric to the beat in the form of a song written by Brian Wilson and Mike Love, 'Surfin'':

'Surfin' is the only life,
The only way for me,
Now surf, surf with me.'

The song became a local hit, and also started a wave of enthusiasm for surf music. There quickly followed a string of national Beach Boy surf hits including 'Surfin' Safari', 'Surfin' USA' and 'Surfer Girl' while with songs like '409', 'Shut Down' and 'Little Deuce Coupe' they started a new craze — hot rod music.

Hot rodding, like surfing, was also a popular West Coast activity. From the illegal street races of the '40s through the Bonneville Salt Flats speed weeks to the sophisticated drag strips of the '60s, it had a long and colourful history. Hot rodding also had its own heroes from customizer George Barris to speed merchant Craig (Spirit Of America) Breedlove, its own publication (Bob Peterson's *Hot Rod* magazine), its own movies and its own music.

For months the Fabulous Forty survey of radio station KFWB listed many surfing and hot rod hits including the Marketts' 'Surfers Stomp' and 'Balboa Blue', the Astronauts' 'Baja', Dick Dale's 'Let's Go Trippin'' and 'The Scavenger', Ronnie and the Daytonas' 'G.T.O.', the Routers' 'Let's Go' and the Trashmen's 'Surfin' Bird' among others.

Southern California at this time was rapidly becoming a nucleus of young talent, all working and helping each other. Five creative songwriters helped keep this new phenomenon active in those early days: Jan Berry, Brian Wilson, Mike Love, Roger Christian and Gary Usher. It was Wilson and Berry who were responsible for the 'Surf City' hit, Wilson and Love for 'Surfin' Safari', Wilson and Christian for 'Little Deuce Coupe' and Wilson and Usher for '409'.

Roger Christian, who rode the discs at KFWB, teamed up with producer and arranger Gary Usher, and like Brian Wilson they consumed every new fad — from hot-rodding, to drag cars and skateboards — that developed out of the West Coast surfing craze. Their songs recorded the social history of their place and times, and their surf song, 'Wax Board And Woodie', included the basic elements of a surfer's life: his car, his freedom, his beach society and the waves.

'I've got a tank full of gas and I'm really
gonna move,
Down to the beach where the surfers
all groove,
Gonna start out before the break of day,
Gonna wax my board then I'm on my way.'

And their hot rod song, 'Hot Rod High':

'Nothing but winners now you losers
scram,
Got no time for a test or a schoolbook
exam,
All the kids know I'm the coolest around,
'Cause I've got the fastest rod in any town,
Now early in the morning I'll be screaming
by,
Loaded up with chicks in front of
Hotrod High.'

Their songs celebrated mindless excitement California-style; man and his love for cars and speed, whether he was on the freeway or riding the waves.

The Usher/Christian songwriting partnership lasted through the surf years supplying songs for various groups and beach movies. Gary Usher also continued his producer/arranger career, contributing to the success of the Hondells' 'Little Honda' and 'My Buddy Seat' hits and many of the Surfaris' recordings while also releasing his own single 'Three Surfer Boys' under the name Gary Usher and the Usherettes.

BRUCE BROWN'S
The Endless Summer

Poster from *The Endless Summer* surf movie.
Right: Late Hawaiian surf champion Duke
Kahanamoku with film maker Bruce Brown.

Jan Berry and Dean Torrence meanwhile had been cutting discs since the late '50s, but they didn't become a major attraction until they moved into the Beach Boys' unique province with the release of an album 'Jan And Dean Take Linda Surfin''. Dean Torrence remembered: "Surfing music had just arrived and Jan and I were physically involved in surfing, so it was natural that we became involved with the music. We had done some hops with the Beach Boys and had sung live with them on numerous occasions. We had enjoyed singing 'Surfin'' and 'Surfin' Safari' with them; we all blended well together." These two songs were featured on the album along with the Beach Boys who loaned their vocal and instrumental support. After the session, Brian Wilson gave them the song 'Surf City', the biggest in a long line of Jan and Dean surf and car hits that included 'Honolulu Lulu', 'Drag City', 'Deadman's Curve', 'The Little Old Lady From Pasadena' and 'Sidewalk Surfin''. Along with the Beach Boys they became the leading group of the surf era.

Wipe Out

The Surfaris were another group on the surf scene, and had a unique blend of both vocal and instrumental surf music. They were still attending high school in their hometown of Glendora, California, when they had their million-seller instrumental hit 'Wipe Out', coupled with a vocal, 'Surfer Joe'. They followed their initial hit with more original singles: 'Point Panic', 'Waikiki Run', 'Scatter Shield' and 'Dune Buggy' but none of these ever had the same impact on the charts — unlike the Rip Chords' 'Hey Little Cobra' which went to the top of the charts under the songwriting/ production auspices of Terry Melcher and Bruce Johnston — who later had two minor hits, 'Custom Machine' and 'Summer Means Fun', under the name of 'Bruce & Terry'.

The Surfaris, however, *did* make it with their albums; 'Wipe Out', 'The Surfaris Play' and the series 'Hit City', 'Fun City USA' all managed to create that special Californian theme they knew so well. Gary Usher stated after arranging and producing one of the 'Hit City' set: "I think their biggest asset is their ability to achieve their recording identity quickly on a session." At their height, the average age of the group — Jim Fuller, Pat Connolly, Bob Berryhill, Jim Pash and Ron Wilson — was only 16.

The Chantays — Brian Carmen, Bob Marshell, Warren Waters, Ron Spickard and Bob Welsh — hailed from Santa Ana and were a close second to the Surfaris as leaders of surf's second division. Sadly, after their much acclaimed hit 'Pipeline' this Californian High School combo failed to make the charts with subsequent releases such as the raunchy single 'Scotch

Top: Troy Donohue and Sandra Dee in a scene from Warner's film *A Summer Place*. Left: Ed Kookie Byrnes from the TV series *77 Sunset Strip*.

Highs'/'Monsoon'. Other Californian surf bands who made the charts included the Fantastic Baggys, featuring Phil Sloan and Steve Barrie, the Challengers, the Sunrays and from further afield, the Astronauts from Boulder, Colorado, the Trashmen from Minneapolis and the Tradewinds from the East Coast.

Beach Movies

American International Pictures were most instrumental in developing the beach movie genre, producing three films a year from 1963–65. Basically they relied on the original hit formula of *Beach Party,* based on or around Malibu beach and directed by William Asher with Frankie Avalon and Annette Funicello heading the cast. This theme produced *Muscle Beach Party, Beach Blanket Bingo, How To Stuff A Wild Bikini, Bikini Beach* and *Ski Party.* They also brought many surf acts to a wider audience, for example Dick Dale and the Del-Tones, Usher and Christian, the Hondells and the Pyramids.

Others were quick to jump on the celluloid surf woodie. The Astronauts and Routers appeared with Bobby Vinton in *Surf Party* and the Beach Boys had star

Above: Surf music's dynamic duo Jan and Dean. Below: The Surfaris, from left to right, Jim Fuller, Jim Pash, Ron Wilson, Bob Berryhill and Pat Connolly.

11

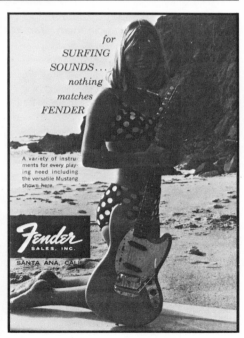

Top left: Fabian in *Ride The Wild Surf*.
Top right: Dick Dale, the Del-Tones and
Stevie Wonder in *Muscle Beach Party*.
Centre: The Astronauts. Bottom left:
Bruce and Terry.

Top: The Beach Boys with Annette Funicello in Disney's *The Monkey's Uncle*. Bottom left: The Hondells in *Ski Party*. Right: Frankie Avalon and Annette Funicello in *Beach Party*.

parts in *Girls On The Beach,* for which they sang the title song. They also turned up in the opening dance sequence of *The Monkey's Uncle,* again singing the title song aided this time by Annette Funicello. The Surfaris sang Terry Melcher's 'Boss Barracuda' in the James Darren/Doug McClure hot rod film *The Lively Set.* Probably the best-remembered beach movie of the period, however, was *Ride The Wild Surf* set in Hawaii. Directed by Don Taylor in 1964, it starred Fabian and Tab Hunter and gave Jan and Dean a hit with the title song. Jan and Dean were to co-star but as Dean Torrence remembered: "Jan and I were supposed to be in this

epic — our film debut co-starring Fabian. But right about the same time a close friend of mine kidnapped Frank Sinatra Jr., so the movie people kicked me out of the film. I think they thought that another one of my friends might try to kidnap Fabian."

Jan and Dean did make their film debut a year later co-hosting the first pop festival movie *The T.A.M.I. Show.* 1965 also saw the emergence of a new West Coast musical trend — folk/rock — and the disappearance of surf music. While the Beach Boys had already outgrown the surf world and were steadily progressing, other groups found they were singing very unsurfy sounds, for example, the Surfaris'

'It Ain't Me Babe' and Jan and Dean's 'Eve Of Destruction'.

It was all over. Bruce Johnston joined the Beach Boys, Terry Melcher and Gary Usher produced the Byrds, Jan Berry had a near fatal car crash, Dean Torrence turned to designing album sleeves and the Rendezvous Ballroom at Balboa burned down. Then, in 1968 the Beach Boys laid on a touch of nostalgia with 'Do It Again':

'Well I've been thinkin 'bout
All the places we've surfed and danced
And all the faces we've missed,
So let's get back together,
And DO IT AGAIN! . . .'

13

The Beach Boys

'Dennis Wilson, toenails tough like brazil nuts, has been surfing for 13 years. It was Dennis Wilson who came out of the water and told Brian what it was like out there. It was Brian who fooled the world.'

(Tom Nolan, *Rolling Stone*, October '71)

Left: The surfin' image with David Marks second from left. Above: Carl, Brian and Dennis Wilson, Mike Love, Al Jardine and dragster.

The Beach Boys are one of the true enigmas of rock. The 'Surf's Up' album, released in October 1971, completed a 10-year cycle for the group ('Surfin'', their first record, was released in October 1961); a 10-year cycle which had seen a somewhat chequered career. The group rose to fame on the wave of enthusiasm for surfing and drag-racing; managed to outlive those crazes by shifting the emphasis of their music to the American/

Californian teenage good life in general; produced one of the most remarkable albums in rock, 'Pet Sounds', only to fall victim to intellectual pretensions. Experimentation with psychedelic drugs, obscure religious sects, the Maharishi and transcendental meditation, health foods, and even an oblique flirtation with Charles Manson, all failed to produce music which would recapture the glory of older days. It took the simple re-discovering of their very life-blood, water, to do that.

The Wilson brothers, Brian, Dennis and Carl, their cousin Mike Love and friend Alan Jardine, all attended high school in Hawthorne, a suburb of San Francisco just five miles from the Pacific Ocean rollers. While Dennis was out surfing, the other four would sit around the house running through Four Freshmen songs. Dennis

loved surfing so much that he persuaded them to form a group together to play music which would be a celebration of the sport. He even came up with the name of the group – Carl and the Passions.

Brian and Mike Love wrote 'Surfin'' for brother Dennis; a simple twelve-bar rock & roll beat. Murry Wilson, the boys' father, was also something of a songwriter himself, and it was his publisher, Hite Morgan, who put the boys on to vinyl. On October 8th, 1961, 'Surfin'' was released on the local Candix label under the name the Beach Boys.

'Surfin'' became quite a sizeable local hit, pushed up to no. 76 in the national Hot 100, and the Beach Boys made their concert debut at the New Year's Eve *Ritchie Valens Memorial Concert* at the Long Beach Municipal Auditorium. The

15

whole music scene at that time was dominated by the East Coast, and Dick Clark's thin-tied Italian singers from Philadelphia and Brooklyn. So, instead of angling the record solely on surfing (a then purely Californian obsession), the Beach Boys tried to cover themselves by introducing a dance into it (Dick Clark's national TV show, *Bandstand*, promoted dances as much as it did Clearasil and Dentyne):

> *From the early early morning,*
> *To the middle of the night*
> *Anytime the surf is up,*
> *The time is right*
> *And when the surf is down,*
> *To take its place*
> *We'll do the surfers' stomp*
> *It's the latest craze.*

Candix thought that the Beach Boys, like 'the surfers' stomp', were simply another craze, a one-hit wonder. Al Jardine did too, and left the group to pursue dentistry. He was replaced by Dave Marks, but returned when the summer, and success, came along. The Candix label itself failed to outlive 'the surfers stomp', and folded, but the group had managed to put down a few more sides including 'Surfin' Safari', 'Surfin' USA' and '409'. Murry Wilson took these around the major record labels without success until he met Nick Venet of Capitol Records, who bought the masters for $300.

In June, 1962, Capitol released 'Surfin' Safari' as the 'B' side to '409' — a song written by Brian Wilson and Gary Usher about Usher's Chevrolet 409. But the American public preferred surfing, even if they were completely land-locked (it says something for its appeal that the record broke first in Phoenix, in the deserts of Arizona). Surfing swept through the nation, and surfing groups sprang up everywhere, even, according to Nick Venet's sleeve notes to 'Surfin' USA', 'in places where the nearest thing to surf is the froth on a chocolate milk shake.'

California Dreaming

After 'Surfin' Safari'/'409' made the Top 10 lists nationally, the Beach Boys clung on to the formula of surfing b/w cars, and five months later 'Surfin' USA'/'Shut Down' repeated the success. 'Surfer Girl'/'Little Deuce Coupe', in August, firmly established the phenomenon of California Dreaming, and the Beach Boys as its leading exponents. At this time the Beach Boys were unashamedly using Chuck Berry's music. Carl Wilson was undoubtedly the best Berry imitator in the business — witness his introduction to 'Fun, Fun, Fun' and his countless guitar breaks, pure Berry. But the Beach Boys weren't content simply to rip off Chuck Berry's riffs, they also borrowed entire songs, particularly 'Sweet Little Sixteen', which was imperceptibly changed to 'Surfin' USA'.

'Surfer Girl'/'Little Deuce Coupe' was the Beach Boys' third national surfing/drag-car hit, after which they wisely abandoned such close identification with

so narrow a life-style. While still retaining the California backdrop of surf, sand, sun and cars, they widened their lyric content to encompass the teenage 'good-life' in general. 'Fun, Fun, Fun' and 'I Get Around' were transition records into the celebration of this American Dream of good times; of school and friend loyalty, of kissing for the first time, of dancing, of girls in general, and of course the hang-ups and heartaches they can bring.

From 1963–65, the Beach Boys poured out hit after hit that paid homage to this life-style: 'Be True To Your School', 'In My Room', 'Don't Worry Baby', 'Barbara Ann', 'All Summer Long', 'Dance, Dance, Dance', 'Do You Want To Dance?', 'Help Me Rhonda', and 'California Girls'. This simple, undemanding music evoked images of the summer sun, waves and girls, open roads and cars; which altogether spelled 'freedom'. The person responsible for all this was Beach Boy Brian Wilson, the oldest of the three brothers. In this period there are two things which mark the music of the Beach Boys: the incredible harmonies of their voices, and the production of the records. Brian Wilson sang lead, arranged all the other voices, and produced their records. Without meaning to demean the talents of the others, during this period he *was* the Beach Boys.

Freedom

Capitol Records, to their credit, recognised the talent that lay within him, and allowed him to produce the group's records — at a time when it was unheard of for a performer to produce himself. When he couldn't find satisfaction within Capitol's own studios, Brian simply used studios, musicians and technicians of his own choice — another unheard of move. At these sessions Brian, who could play almost every instrument himself, would show each session musician what to play. In the process he wasn't only singing about freedom, but actually giving it to musicians in California, and subsequently the whole of the rock industry. The more he worked, the more sophisticated Brian became in his production techniques. The progression can be seen simply enough from 'Don't Worry Baby', through 'Help Me Rhonda' and 'Do You Want To Dance?' to the brilliant 'California Girls' — which used brass and organ prominently for the first time. This increasing sophistication of production techniques was paralleled by Brian's increased dissatisfaction with the lyric content and style of their records. His ideas were not being adequately expressed in either his own lyrics or those of the lyricists he used. It was time to put away the surfboard wax — the wave had been ridden long enough.

Because of several nervous breakdowns caused through over-work, Brian Wilson decided to stop touring with the group. "I used to be Mr. Everything", he explained, "I felt I had no choice. I was run down mentally and emotionally because I was running around jumping on jets from one

city to another on one-night stands, also producing, writing, arranging, singing, planning, teaching — to the point where I had no peace of mind, and no chance to actually sit down and think or even rest."

Death Blow

Naturally enough, the other guys in the group — and indeed the world — saw this as the death-blow to the Beach Boys. But Brian had it all worked out, and he convinced the rest of the group that he would still carry on working and singing with them . . . he just wouldn't, *couldn't*, go on those energy-sapping tours. Reconciled to his decision, the group took on a local studio musician by the name of Glenn Campbell, as Brian's touring substitute. But he didn't work out so well, and after about four months Mike Love brought in Bruce Johnston. They'd known Bruce for a couple of years, since the days when he was producing over at Columbia, and had been the 'Bruce' in another California surfing group Bruce and Terry — the 'Terry' being Terry Melcher of Byrds, Raiders, Doris Day and Charles Manson fame. Bruce fitted in perfectly, and was to stay with them through to 1972 and just after 'Surf's Up'.

While the others were touring Brian wasn't wasting his time, and the year's breathing space it had given him enabled him to develop so much that with their next album they produced one of the milestones of rock music, 'Pet Sounds'. Brian had always been a devotee of Phil Spector, and the progression through 'Don't Worry Baby', 'Help Me Rhonda' and 'California Girls' had been a process of synthesising Spector's production techniques with the raunchy rock music of the Beach Boys. With 'Pet Sounds' this synthesis was complete.

'Pet Sounds' marked a complete abandonment of the Beach Boys' music (1962–65). No longer was it enough to be concerned only with the next wave or the new set of tyres or even the problems of adolescent love; the world had far wider horizons, and far more meaningful relationships (the opening track, 'Wouldn't It Be Nice?' explicitly extolled the simple pleasures of sleeping together). 'Pet Sounds' retained all those intricate vocal harmonies, but matched them with more ambitious structures — not too ambitious, but a decided advance on the 'two-verse/chorus/instrumental-break/chorus' formula of the past. The instrumentation was more advanced, and used a much wider range of instruments and styles and sound effects. The album even had two orchestrated tracks, and overlooking Brian's tendency to overdo the lush production, the album was near-faultless. Brian himself wrote all 13 tracks, collaborating on 8 of them with Tony Asher. It was to be the maturation of not only the Beach Boys, but the whole American rock movement.

Capitol Records, however, didn't want the Beach Boys to mature into the Beach Men; after all, as boys they'd been turning out hit after predictable hit, so why change? At first they even refused to issue it, and it was only after a long-protracted battle that they did eventually release it — while at the same time re-issuing their old hits on 'The Best Of The Beach Boys', and giving it a preferential promotion.

Brian Wilson is a very sensitive guy, prone to nervous breakdowns. He'd worked on the album for almost a year, so when Capitol rejected it he was deeply affected, and its eventual release didn't do much to alter that. 'Pet Sounds' was a critical success, but not (understandably in the circumstances) a commercial one, although three of the tracks became big singles hits: 'Wouldn't It Be Nice?', 'Sloop John B' and 'God Only Knows'.

Own Label

The rift with Capitol and the subsequent critical acclaim of 'Pet Sounds' had two important consequences. The group decided to form their own record label, and to leave Capitol. They wanted to do so immediately, but after some strong legal words they agreed to work out their contract, but no more. (Their following album, 'Smiley Smile' was on their Brother Records label, but distributed through Capitol. They had to give up three more albums before they could go fully independent, which they did with the 'Sunflower' album).

Critics began to acclaim Brian as a genius, but this was something which disturbed him. He had always been 'eccentric', to say the least, and when he received the blessing of the nascent underground/flower movement in California, he started to go through all the many different trips and crazes they embraced — but at super-speed. Brian Wilson has often been described as a 'total' person, meaning that when he commits himself, he goes the whole way. The first four years of the Beach Boys had given him the money to indulge in anything that took his fancy; so, when he suddenly had a craze on basketball, the main room in his house was converted into a gymnasium; when he wanted to play the piano with his feet in the sand, the room was filled up with sand. The stories of Brian's eccentricity just go on and on — living in a tent in the living room, holding business meetings in his outdoor swimming pool, at night, wanting to open a 24-hour table tennis shop because he found he couldn't buy equipment at three in the morning . . .

Brian also went through the more serious eccentricities of the time, LSD and other drugs. He enlisted the help of Van Dyke Parks during this period, and they began work on an album which was to be called 'Smile'. In November of 1966, while deeply immersed in the album, 'Good Vibrations' was released. It had taken six months to make (at one point Brian decided not to release it) and cost $16,000. It was the Beach Boys' biggest hit of all time, and their first million-seller. The laurels marked 'genius' started piling up outside Brian's door, unnerving him in his current project.

While he and Van Dyke Parks were making the album in the studios, the Beach Boys were out touring Europe. When they returned they were astounded by the sounds they heard, and rejected it. They couldn't comprehend the Van Dyke Parks lyrics, they argued that such studio-based music with orchestras and all couldn't be reproduced on stage, and they couldn't relate to the very advanced studio techniques and use of effects — this in pre-'Sgt. Pepper' days.

This rift within the group hampered the completion of the album, and when Brian was forced to concentrate on 'Heroes And Villains' — one of the 'Smile' tracks — as the single follow-up to 'Good Vibrations', things began to disintegrate. Van Dyke Parks left, and the release of 'Sgt. Pepper' sealed the project's fate. But the 'Smile' music wasn't all lost, and most of it has turned up on various post-'Pet Sounds' albums: 'Surf's Up' on the album of the same name; 'Cabinessence' '20/20'; and the bulk of it, including 'Heroes And Villains', 'Vegetables', 'Wonderful' and 'Wind Chimes', on the 'Smiley Smile' album.

Warmth And Humour

At the insistence of Capitol, 'Good Vibrations' was also included on 'Smiley Smile', which turned out to be a very under-rated album. It has a high critical reputation now, and is used by some drug-therapy clinics in the States. The making of 'Smiley Smile' as a good album was not so much the individually brilliant tracks such as 'Good Vibrations' and 'Heroes And Villains', as the general warmth and humour which came through as a result of those unique Beach Boy harmonies. Much of the album is purely vocal with the very minimum of instrumentation, and it was a high-point in Brian Wilson's use of the voice as an instrument.

In the meantime, Brian had moved into his Bel-Air Mansion with its own studio. The first album to come out of it was 'Wild Honey', released only two months after 'Smiley Smile'. 'Wild Honey' seemed in many ways to be an album aimed at patching up the damaged relations within the group itself, with its deceptively simple music firmly back in the rhythm & blues vein and several of the tracks co-written by Brian and Mike Love, who had been his sternest critic as regards the 'new music'. In fact Wilson Love wrote 10 of the 11 tracks on 'Wild Honey', including the album's two masterpieces, 'Wild Honey' and 'Country Air'. In many ways 'Country Air' is the perfect Beach Boys track of all-time in both style and content. The merciless singing of their voices blends superbly with their own instrumentation, while still retaining the orchestral 'wave' and mixing in the lone sound effect of a cock crowing.

The brief lyrics too are simple but evocative:

Top left: Bruce Johnston. Right: The Beach Boys in London. Below: Celebrating 15 years in the business.

Get a breath of that country air
Breathe the beauty of the everywhere
Get a look at that clear blue sky

But 'Wild Honey' failed to lift them back into the 'Good Vibrations' league of popularity, as did their subsequent albums 'Friends' (Brian's personal favourite album and their first stereo one), '20/20' and 'Sunflower' (which was their first after breaking away from Capitol). Perhaps a reason was the lack of a distinct image for the group, which had by now completely lost its surfing label, but had simply replaced it with a succession of others, each changing from album to album. "They've been trying to get away from the beach, you know?" said Van Dyke Parks: "They don't like their image. Even when I first ran into them I could never figure out why. What's wrong with it? Get them down to the beach. Put them into trunks. The beach ain't so bad. The ocean is the repository of the entire human condition — the pollution, the solution . . . "

Pollution

Van Dyke Parks was shown to be right. 'Sunflower' ended on the right note with 'Cool Cool Water' and the 'Surf's Up' album, which followed it, started with 'Don't Go Near The Water' (by Al Jardine). Much of the 'Surf's Up' album dealt with water and environmental pollution in general. And it was this album which lifted them back into cult status of the 'Good Vibrations' order. The Beach Boys re-discovered water, and the rock movement re-discovered them. Perhaps the attraction to the album was the inclusion of the title track, a song by Brian and Van Dyke Parks from the ill-fated 'Smile' album; or perhaps it was simply the

brilliant album cover that sold the record.

In the event, 'Surf's Up' proved to be a very important album for several reasons. First, it saw the first collaborations of Brian (and the others) with Jack Rieley, a former reporter for NBC news, former producer for Pacifica Radio, who had become something nebulous in their management, co-ordinator of the press office and, of course, lyricist. Rieley even sang lead vocal on one of the tracks, 'A Day In The Life Of A Tree', which he had written with Brian. Secondly, the album saw the demise of Brian's influence as major songwriter and producer. Only the last three songs on the album were by him, two very short and the last one, 'Surf's Up' quite a few years old. All the other Beach Boys had songs on it, even Carl who had never written before. Most of the songs by the other Beach Boys were successful, notably Bruce Johnston's 'Disney Girls (1957)', and Mike Love's 'Student Demonstration Time' (a re-wording of Leiber and Stoller's 'Riot In Cell Block Number 9'), in which his voice was distorted to give a 'megaphone' effect, and police sirens were, with amazing success, used as instruments. But the attention of the album centred on Carl, his successful tracks, particularly 'Feel Flows', and his talents as a producer.

After the release of 'Surf's Up', Bruce Johnston (the only one not into transcendental meditation and health foods) left and Ricky Fataar and Blondie Chaplin from Flame, a South African group the Beach Boys had signed, came in. Dennis' right hand was badly cut in an accident, and he couldn't drum or contribute very effectively any longer.

With these changes, the internal structure of the Beach Boys broke down. The first album of this radically new line-up

was the very disappointing 'Carl And The Passions: So Tough'. The superb art-work and titling on the cover gave the impression of consolidating the return to earlier sentiments, as did the title, which was their original name. But the whole album was the worst for a long time, and clearly showed the fate of Brian's producing. Only one track stood out above the mediocrity, and that was Dennis Wilson and Jack Rieley's 'Marcella'.

Return To Their Roots

The group moved away to Amsterdam for a while and recorded their 'Holland' album there. It was a great improvement on 'Carl And The Passions', and Alan Jardine's 'California Saga: California' particularly was heralded as a return to their roots. Again Brian Wilson's role was cut back, to just two tracks — 'Sail On Sailor' (another Van Dyke Parks collaboration) and 'Funky Pretty' — and to the 7-inch record enclosed, which was a fairy tale called 'Mount Vernon And Fairway'.

Then, following a series of successful live gigs in Southern California, came the double-album 'In Concert' set spanning the group's history all the way from 'Surfer Girl' to 'Sail On Sailor'. Although the album was itself well received, the really good news came with the announcement that Flames Blondie Chaplin and Ricky Fataar had left — leaving the Beach Boys with their original 1961 line-up.

In 1976, the Beach Boys released an album called '15 Big Ones' in celebration of an important anniversary. It was 15 years since their initial record success in 1961 and the five Beach Boys were still together, producing that unique style of music that has made them one of the world's most original groups.

SUNSHINE & SMOG

The City of the Angels, long a centre for movies and TV, also harboured an important recording industry which attracted—as Hollywood always had—young hopefuls from all over the States. It became a musical melting pot for many varied styles and home for a wide range of artists as diverse as The Byrds and Joni Mitchell, The Mamas & Papas and The Doors, Alice Cooper and Nilsson.

Greater Los Angeles' 10 million inhabitants live in what must have been one of the most comfortable spots on earth . . . until *they* arrived. Now the abundant sunshine filters through the diesel fumes and the mediterranean plain is awash with concrete freeways and gigantic shopping complexes. One of the world's highest suicide rates holds hands with the stars walking down Hollywood Boulevard. Kerouac, crouching in his railroad yard in *Dharma Bums,* wrote, 'the smog was heavy, my eyes weeping from it, the sun was hot, the air stank, a regular hell is LA'.

And yet the comfort is still there. LA has the reputation of being a both relaxing and creative environment. Many of its musicians have said that they couldn't write or live anywhere else. LA is the ultimate urban achievement with all that that implies for good and bad. Business-

wise it's certainly the place to be. The movie, TV, and music businesses have grown up together and filled the city with people dedicated to the financial success of art. Everyone in the music business comes to LA because more acts are discovered there, and because more records are cut there than in most of the rest of the world put together.

The movie/TV connection has left LA with a musical tradition of attention to topicality, and a devotion to production craftsmanship. In the early '60s these concerns were being lavished on the surfin'/hot-rod records of the Beach Boys, Jan and Dean, and hundreds of lesser-known groups. The sound was immaculately smooth and sunny, conjuring across the nation an image of paradise on Malibu Beach. But by 1965, surfin' wasn't as topical as Vietnam, and elsewhere the music was getting 'serious' via the Beatles and Dylan. The Byrds' achievement was to synthesise these two and LA into a new mainstream, known as folk-rock.

The Byrds are dealt with at length elsewhere in this history. They brought together folk and rock, East and West

coast, and in particular the new phenomenon of the dope and sunshine politics of love, descendants of the beats and precursors of the hippies. It was a new blend and a dynamic one. In early 1965 they started playing the clubs in LA, particularly Ciro's. In April, former surf-writer Terry Melcher took McGuinn and the old LA session crew into the studio to cut Dylan's 'Mr. Tambourine Man'. Folk-rock was born, and boomed.

In the autumn of 1965, John and Michelle Phillips, Cass Elliot and Denny Doherty, arrived in LA as folkie exiles from Greenwich Village. They ran into Barry McGuire, who that summer had hit the jackpot with the classically crass 'Eve Of Destruction', and he in turn introduced them to his producer Lou Adler, a friend of Brian Wilson and former producer of Jan and Dean and Johnny Rivers. Adler recognised their potential, but knowing that folk, as such, wouldn't make it, he recruited the LA session-men — Osborn, Knetchel, Blaine, Glen Campbell — to back the group on sessions. As Jerry Hopkins wrote, 'it was simple, obvious, but it produced the unique Mamas and Papas

LOVE

Above: Publicist Derek Taylor flanked by Byrds Gene Clark and Chris Hillman and actor Peter Fonda. Right: Songwriter/producer Van Dyke Parks. Left: The harmonious Harpers Bizarre.

sound – California beat meeting Greenwich Village Melody, as perfect a marriage of styles as the Byrds had produced earlier'.

Their first hit, and a huge one, was 'California Dreamin''. It was the new LA sound – the careful interweaving of vocal harmonies with a sunshine beat, the joy of a generation literally on the move, and the power of their dream set against the reality outside. The singer laments winter in New York, thinking that if he was in LA he could go out for a walk in the sun. This wishful thinking is turned by the joy of the melody and performance into something ultimately stronger than the reality.

Two Sides Of The Coin

The contest between hope and reality is where LA rock tended to begin and end. But Phillips is a gifted writer, and hidden amongst the joy of 'California Dreamin'' is another edge:

'I dropped into a church
I passed along the way
You know the preacher loves the cold
He knows I'm gonna stay . . . '

The reality and the hope (the cold and the church) are two sides of the same coin. How to lose one without the other?

Through 1965–67 the group had a string of hits – 'Monday Monday', 'Creeque Alley', 'Dedicated To The One I Love' – all of which followed roughly the same formula, a joyous sound with a cautionary gentle sting. But eventually the Mamas and Papas became so involved with the Flower Power movement that they faded with it. Their importance was in tying together pop and folk into something of more than merely immediate value. When the 'political life' of the music of 1965–67 split into factions, in LA and elsewhere, the music and its audience did also. The group's last hit record, 'Safe In My Garden', was a sign of the times. A far more muted sound, verging on the beautiful melancholy to come from the likes of Neil Young and Van Morrison in 1968–69, it looked back on recent riots on the Strip a little sadder and a little wiser. Perhaps their best record, it was their smallest hit. The Mamas and Papas had been left in a vacuum – too sweet for the heavies, too heavy for the sweets.

While the Mamas and Papas were happy 'dreaming', a new group appeared on the Strip. Led by two former UCLA (University of California, LA) film students, Jim Morrison and Ray Manzarek, the Doors represented a harder side to LA rock. It was still smooth, but it was also raw and theatrical. Morrison himself was almost an American Jagger, black leather and sex, exaggerated to the brink of parody.

The crucial thing about the Doors' music was the 'political' drive behind it. More than any other LA group, and with more subtlety than any of the Frisco groups to come, they spoke for the new consciousness and the need to 'break on through', to 'learn to forget'. Morrison himself wrote poetic lyrics, and was an admirer of Artaud's

'Theatre of Cruelty'. This was best exemplified in the two long tracks that closed their first two albums. 'The End' was a coherent exploration of breaking on through. Dark and convulsive, studded with images of a world on the edge, its spoken oedipal section – 'kill the father, rape the mother' – went somewhat beyond the clichés of 'doing one's own thing' currently in fashion. The 'end' was two-edged, the joy of breaking through and the pain of wrenching out one's ego:

'This is the end, beautiful friend
This is the end, my only friend, the end
The end of laughter and soft lies
The end of nights we tried to die'

'When The Music's Over' was one of the first songs to explicitly identify the new rock as a means to something else. Music was a special friend, until the end. And that end – 'We want the world and we want it . . . NOW'.

In The Name Of Love

In one of the Byrds' early audiences at Ciro's was Arthur Lee. Recently he said, 'I saw the Byrds and they really flipped me out because their music really hit my heart. Up until I heard the Byrds, everything was rhythm & blues. And they were doing their own material, and it sounded like the music I wrote on my own, you know what I mean?'. Lee went away and formed a group called the Grass Roots, and started to play the clubs. Discovering that another group had somehow got first rights on the name, he soon changed it to Love.

In the meantime the Elektra record company was busy looking for a folk-rock act to shake loose their folk-purist reputation. Jac Holzman, the head of the label, saw Love at Bido Lito's in the early summer of 1965, and eventually signed them up. Their first two records in 1966, 'Love' and 'De Capo', featured a strange mutation of the Byrds and R&B, as if the rough edges of the latter had been smoothed out by the style of the former. It was the third record though, 'Forever Changes', which became a classic. Beautiful flowing sounds of acoustic strumming, muted electric leads, velvet brass and gently sweeping strings – all topped by lyrics that dealt in nihilistic despair. R&B was as absent from the music as folk-rock was from the words. In its rampant schizophrenia, this album stands out as 'Classic' LA.

Folk-rock had taken from Dylan the romantic expressionism of 'Mr. Tambourine Man'. Lee, though, took the closing options and claustrophobia of 'It's Alright Ma'. On the 'Forever Changes' cover Lee stands with a mocking 'how do *you* feel?' look on his face, holding the two halves of a broken vase full of dead flowers.

'You think you're happy
And you are happy
That's what you're happy for'

Lee's lyrical technique was often to play

on words, twisting them around until the emptiness beneath is exposed.

He consistently uses titles to give songs a completely new reference point, for example calling a gentle song about humming birds and girls with pigtails, 'The Good Humour Man He Sees Everything Like This'. Lastly, he plays endlessly on the theme of time so loved by the surrealist tradition. 'Time time time . . . ' he sings, keeping time.

Love broke away from the LA tradition of performing badly outside LA by the simple expedient of not moving more than three miles from their old horror movie set/house outside Hollywood. There they reportedly consumed large quantities of drugs and threw the telephone across the room when it rang. After 'Forever Changes' they recorded another album which was apparently too awful to release, and then they split. Lee continues to this day, turning out less mellow music with much the same surreal lyrics. But the blend of 'Forever Changes' has never since been repeated, the blend that somehow typified LA – the smooth ride into nowhere under the name of Love.

The number of musicians passing through LA in 1965–67 was immense. Two of them, together with two actors, were turned into the Monkees for a TV series. Their records were hugely successful, threatening at one point to raise the sought-after spectre of Beatlemania. In their conception and musical essence they differed little from more recent LA/TV creations like *The Partridge Family*, but in the style of their TV shows they were remarkably different. Apeing the Beatle films, the shows were surrealism for the teenybopper, and way ahead of their time.

Heavier groups too, like Steppenwolf, Clear Light, and Iron Butterfly, were all touched by LA's mellow politicism, as were the rock/blues groups like Canned Heat and Spirit.

Chimes And Harmonies

Meanwhile the folkies tended toward rhythm, just as the rockers tended toward melody. Crosby produced the first record by the lady now arguably LA's brightest star, Joni Mitchell. On that record Stephen Stills played bass. His own group, the Buffalo Springfield, had arrived rather late on the LA scene, and perhaps for that reason summed it up as well as anyone. *Crawdaddy* editor Paul Williams, writing about them once said: 'there's love in their music – not the driving evangelical love of the Airplane, but a straight forward take-it-or-leave-it love, all yours if you want it and will share in it'. Electric virtuosity was reduced to a minimum, guitars chimed rather than cut, and soft harmonies were more frequent than the lusty howl.

Of those who'd been in LA before it all happened, the old session crews backed the folk-rockers just as they'd backed the surfers before. Some of them, like Glen Campbell and Leon Russell, eventually became big stars on their own. The

Buffalo Springfield, the embryo of many supergroups of the future.

premiere group of the Surf Era were as much a part of the new scene as they had been of the old one. Brian Wilson devoted himself to being a genius, pitched a tent in his living room, created 'Pet Sounds' and 'Good Vibrations', and brought a new intricacy to the Beach Boys' harmonising and a new beauty to rock music.

And of course many other acts had emerged in the folk-rock mainstream – the Turtles, Kaleidoscope, Harpers Bizarre, Spanky and our Gang – all appearing at the larger ballrooms like the Cheetah, Kaleidoscope and Shrine Exposition, and at the smaller clubs like the Troubador, Ash Grove, Golden Bear, and Whiskey A Go Go. David Gates, now of 'Bread' fame, was connected with Randy Newman, Van Dyke Parks and Jack Nitzsche, with producer Lenny Waronker, and with the huge Metric Music publishing house. Duane Allman was playing with a group called Hourglass. And the lovable madmen, from Kim Fowley to Captain Beefheart via Tiny Tim and Frank Zappa, were alternately making the scene and breaking it up. It all hung together in a unifying LA style and stance. Someone once told the then folk singer Tim Buckley that he was like a

character out of a Scott Fitzgerald novel. "There's a lot of us about," he said.

The music scene of 1965–67 reflected and was reflected by the social changes accompanying it. Drugs were available in quantity and everyone wore beads. In LA, as elsewhere, head shops proliferated, and along with the underground press and clubs changed hands and names with great frequency.

But in late 1966 and early '67 the LA police (the 'Heat') moved in. Demonstrators were hauled away in the paddy wagons, and full-scale riots erupted several times. The police moved in on the head shops and clubs, prosecuting on the slightest pretext. Outside LA the long hot summers of '66 and '67 led inexorably through the Battle of Chicago to the election of Nixon as President; and in LA Robert Kennedy was shot dead in June 1968.

The music of thoughtful hope emanating from LA was more likely to be affected by all this than the music of half-blind hope blaring out of San Francisco. Two LA songs which investigated the Strip riots were indicative of the change coming over the music there. Stephen Stills' 'For What It's

Worth' asked all the right sort of questions, without posing any facile answers. Demonstrating was just 'a field-day for the Heat'. And paranoia was no way to love. But it was in the general sound that this record in some way marked a turning-point. Its smoothness was more ominous than relaxed. Hope with a tinge of caution was giving way to resignation with a touch of hope. The balance was shifting.

Getting out, as Peter Fonda and Dennis Hopper found in *Easy Rider*, was not so easy. The movie, from the setting to the music, summed up the state of the LA scene. It didn't have a happy ending. By 1968 flower power was virtually dead, and the focus had moved conclusively away to San Francisco. LA music split anew into compartments, with a new mainstream to show for the previous years. The Mamas and Papas and Love faded away, the Doors marked time up to the crowning blow of Jim Morrison's death. The Byrds and the Springfield split into new Byrds, Poco, Burrito Brothers, CSN&Y, Loggins and Messina, ad apparently infinitum.

The new input was, logically enough in the ultimate city, country music. Gene Clark left the Byrds early, and led the way with the Gosdin Brothers and then Doug Dillard of the Dillards. The Byrds, with country freak Gram Parsons replacing Dave Crosby, followed. Then Hillman and Parsons left the Byrds to form the Burritos and take it all a stage further on.

On the other side of the divide, the same old session-crew were backing a new generation of singer/songwriters in the acoustic revival that started around 1970. Lou Adler was in the act again with Carole King. Waronker was producing Gordon Lightfoot; Randy Newman and Van Dyke Parks were making their own records. Various Byrds and Buffaloes were becoming superstars with the new acoustic/electric 'gotta-get-down-to-it-but-it's-hard' mainstream – living in Laurel and Topanga Canyons and insisting that they were only musicians.

By 1970, the coincidence of seriousness and melody, which had sold LA records had disappeared. Practically no one out-standing has appeared since, most of the big names on the 1965–67 scene are still the big names now, older and perhaps playing a little wearily with the tradition they created. Gene Clark, with as good a claim as anyone to have started the ball rolling, recently wrote a song, 'LA Freeway', that echoes the 'Mr. Tambourine Man' of 1965, but with a sad desperation that was never in the early Byrds. The words, though, would have been as apposite then as they are now:

'If I can just get off of that LA freeway
Without getting killed or caught
Down the road in a cloud of smoke
For some land that I ain't bought, bought,
bought
If I can just get off of that LA freeway . . .'

THE BYRDS

'Won't you pay for your riches and
fame?
Was it all a strange game? You're a
little insane,
Money that came and the public
acclaim
Don't forget what you are, you're
a rock'n'roll star.'

('So You Wanna Be A Rock'n'Roll Star?')

So sang the Byrds in 1967 in a song
riddled with irony. After two years of
success, a year as international chart
toppers and a year as an 'established'
group, 1967 saw the Byrds as has-beens.
The dubbed-on screams were real, but
they came from a 1965 concert; no one
was screaming at the Byrds in '67.

A further level of irony is that back in the

early '60s, when the various soon-to-be-
Byrds were making their first tentative
steps in the music business, rock & roll
stardom was the last thing that they
sought. For Jim (later Roger) McGuinn,
Dave Crosby, Chris Hillman, Gene Clark
and Michael Clarke — in common with
many others — rock & roll was dead. It
was in folk that most of the Byrds began

their musical careers. McGuinn, the only
one with a musical education, started
backing the Limeliters, joined the Chad
Mitchell Trio, and then in 1962 began
doing folk music session work and
supporting Bobby Darin, who had introduced a folk spot into his night-club act.
Similarly, Gene Clark did a stint with the
New Christy Minstrels, and Crosby was a
Les Baxter Balladeer for a while (Baxter
was a big-time American band leader, who
in the wake of the folk boom, like Darin,
quickly inserted a folk slot in his show).
Hillman, like McGuinn, began playing folk
in local coffee houses, then temporarily
left folk for bluegrass, first with the
Scottsville Squirell Breakers and then
with his own group, the Hillmen, as a joint

S.I./Peter Owen

27

Above: Byrds 1965 — Chris Hillman, David Crosby, Gene Clark, Jim McGuinn, Mike Clarke (unseen). Centre picture: Byrds 1965 again — Mike Clarke, Jim McGuinn, Chris Hillman, David Crosby, Gene Clark — and Bob Dylan, whose songs the Byrds remade, adding their own distinct formula at that time.

folk and bluegrass venture of some merit.

By 1964, the Byrds as individuals were almost old troupers on the folk scene. Like rock & roll before it, folk was being swallowed up by the record industry. In McGuinn's words: "It was getting very commercial and plastic packaged in cellophane . . . a low quality product . . . I wanted to get into something else."

The opportunity to form a group came when McGuinn played the Troubadour in LA in the summer of 1964. Gene Clark saw him, and suggested they form a group — 24 hours later Crosby joined them and they began rehearsing as the Jet Set. Stuck in LA on their own, they turned for help to Jim Dickson, who had tried recording Crosby as a solo singer and was also trying to sell an album he'd produced for the Hillmen. When it became apparent that the Jet Set wouldn't make it as a trio, Dickson asked Hillman to join. He did, and so all that was needed now was a drummer — enter Mike Clarke, a conga-playing acquaintance of Crosby's.

Songs On Tape

The next step was to get some material together and go looking for a recording contract. Since Dickson had the run of World Pacific studios they decided to make a tape of their songs. McGuinn later described their early music as a synthesis of Dylan and the Beatles:

"In the spectrum of music at the time . . .

I saw this gap, with Dylan and the Beatles leaning towards each other in concept. That's where we aimed."

But when the tapes were eventually released as 'Preflyte', the lame 'Little Drummer Boy' version of 'Mr. Tambourine Man' notwithstanding, it was the Beatles influence, not to mention imitation, that stood out.

On the basis of this tape Dickson got them a 'one record and option' deal with Elektra for which, billed as the Beefeaters ("I plead guilty . . . but there had been such a run of British groups," Jac Holzman, then president of Elektra) they put out a very Beatlish single 'Please Let Me Love You' in the autumn of 1964. The record failed, and the band, now officially the Byrds, switched to Columbia (CBS). Once again the search for a single began. Earlier that year the Animals had had hits with 'Baby Let Me Take You Down' and 'House Of The Rising Sun', which were rocked-up Dylan material, if not Dylan compositions, so Dickson suggested they remake 'Mr. Tambourine Man'. They did (with the help of session-men Hal Blaine, Leon Russell and Larry Knetchel), and after a six-month wait for it to be released it soared to the top of both the US and British charts.

Like 'Satisfaction', 'Like A Rolling Stone' and 'She Loves You', 'Mr. Tambourine Man' is one of rock's great singles, but in 1965, its significance lay more in what it represented: the arrival of folk rock and the

stemming of the tide of the British Invasion. Though the Byrds rose to success with the song and the freaky image they projected, they faded quickly. Their second record, 'All I Really Want To Do', was beaten to the top by a Sonny and Cher cover version, and, though their next, 'Turn! Turn! Turn!'; made no. 1 in October 1965, from then on they were always struggling for chart success.

Diamonds Of Perfection

In the two years between 'Mr. Tambourine Man' and 'Eight Miles High' the Byrds changed a lot. After their first success Columbia allowed the band to play on the follow-up album, which was the expected synthesis of Dylan, 'folk' songs and their own compositions. But if the material was straight folk-rock, their performance of it showed the first real signs that 'Mr. Tambourine Man' was no accident. On all the songs the Byrds made an attempt to stylise and Byrdise the material. By the next album, 'Turn! Turn! Turn!', the Byrds had got folk-rock down pat: out of songs like Gene Clark's 'Set You Free This Time', Dylan's 'Lay Down Your Weary Tune' and the traditional title song, the Byrds created little diamonds of formal perfection. All that was missing was a sense of excitement.

The next album, 'SD', demonstrated that the Byrds were certainly weary of folk-rock. In between it and 'Turn', Gene

CBS

Top picture: Byrds 1968 — Kevin Kelley, Gram Parsons, Roger McGuinn, Chris Hillman. Bottom row, left: Byrds 1967 — Jim McGuinn, David Crosby, Chris Hillman, Mike Clarke. Right: Byrds 1967 — Mike Clarke, Chris Hillman, David Crosby, Jim McGuinn.

Clark had quit to pursue a solo career, thus causing McGuinn and Crosby to either write more songs (Clark had been the group's major songwriter) or look further outside the group than Dylan for material. Strangely, the result was the first Byrds album without any Dylan songs. In their place were very traditional folk songs ('Wild Mountain Tyme'), and the beginnings of McGuinn's personal space odyssey in which science and mysticism were equally mixed ('Mr. Spaceman', '5D'). '5D', which was issued as a single and bombed completely, made explicit the gap between the group's concerns and those of their audience:

'Oh how is it that I could come out to here
And be still floating,
And never hit bottom and keep falling
  through
Just relaxed and paying attention?'

At a time when 'Eight Days A Week' was a surrealist idea for most record buyers, McGuinn wanted his fans to understand and *buy* a record that he later explained '. . . as an ethereal trip into metaphysics . . .'

On the singles McGuinn *was* the Byrds: it was his voice and distinctive guitar that were the group's trademarks. On the albums however, McGuinn was merely one of the group. 'Younger Than Yesterday', the fourth album, saw Hillman and Crosby step forward. The album was released just after 'Sgt. Pepper', and was wholly overshadowed by it. Moreover it was made at the time when the Byrds were at their lowest ebb. As Crosby explained:

''The Byrds would come out there and be a mechanical wind-up-doll. . . . We would get through a set, forty minutes long — just barely — of material that we had done so many times we were ready to throw up with it. We were bored; we were uptight.''

Baroque Rock

Yet, following up their tradition of capping each album with the next one, 'Younger' saw the electronic experimentation of '5D' brought to absolute perfection: 'CTA 102', a McGuinn space-song about a quasar, caught the sounds of space to a T, 'Have You Seen Her Face?', and 'Time Between' saw Hillman out-do the Beatles, while Crosby on 'Everybody's Been Burned' and 'Renaissance Fair' proved himself a master of baroque rock and, of course, there was 'So You Want To Be A Rock'n'Roll Star'.

Crosby, by this time fed up with the bad gigs and bad feeling inside the group, was forever threatening to leave and showing his feelings by gigging with Buffalo Springfield when they opened the show for the Byrds — a very unprofessional thing to do.

The crisis came to a head in late 1967, during the recording of the next album, 'The Notorious Byrd Brothers'. Crosby refused to sing Goffin King 'pop' songs — 'Goin' Back' and 'Wasn't Born To Follow' — demanded more political songs, and then finally quit for a cash settlement to join Crosby, Stills and Nash — leaving the group with a half-completed album. Somehow the Byrds managed to finish it as a trio, and again somehow it was superb. More importantly, for the Byrds at least, the group had a lucky break. Classified as a singles group by the new rock audience that had suddenly appeared in 1967, 'Younger Than Yesterday' had been neglected as an album. But by the time of 'The Notorious Byrd Brothers' in 1968, the growing number of rock *critics* had begun to re-appraise the Byrds, and thus gave the album a good reception and it sold fairly well. Moreover, the same audience that couldn't understand 'Eight Miles High' would quite happily accept 'Change Is Now'.

By now the Byrds had a growing cult following, though the larger audience raised on San Francisco music still eluded the band. To capture that audience another 'Notorious' was required. Instead, the Byrds added Gram Parsons and replaced Mike Clarke with Kevin Kelley and headed up country with 'Sweetheart Of The Rodeo'. The Byrds just couldn't stand still for long enough to collect an audience around them. Later, 'Sweetheart' would be seen as enormously influential,

but in 1968, no one in either the States or Britain was willing to accept any rock group, let alone the Byrds, singing Merle Haggard redneck songs.

But if 'Sweetheart Of The Rodeo' lost the Byrds the progressive album audience, it also more or less destroyed the band. The next time the group came to record, McGuinn would be the only original member left. First Gram Parsons left when the Byrds agreed to do a tour of South Africa, and then on their return, when McGuinn wanted out of the country trip, Hillman, who's idea it had been, left to form the Flying Burrito Brothers with . . . Gram Parsons. McGuinn had always been the group's front-man but, never very good at handling break-ups, he seemed about to lose all credibility as Crosby sneered at him from the safety of CSN: ''As far as I'm concerned there were only five Byrds ever. Period.'' Leaving Hillman to deal the killing blow: ''All McGuinn's doing now is riding it out till it ends, just for the money.''

Easy Rider

The new, new Byrds' album, 'Dr. Byrds And Mr. Hyde', with Gene Parsons (no relation) on drums, Clarence White on guitar and John York on bass, didn't help McGuinn much: first it was pretty bad, and second he seemed unable to get away from country musicians. Henceforth, like it or not, there would always be a country tinge to the Byrds' music. At this low point luck entered the picture again in the

30

form of the film *Easy Rider,* which used a few of their songs on the soundtrack. The Byrds were almost respectable again. The album that quickly followed, 'Ballad Of Easy Rider', was better than average and against all predictions, the Byrds seemed to be on the way up again.

By 1970, Skip Battin (of Skip and Flip, an early '60s imitation Everly Brothers) had replaced John York, and after some hard touring the group even began to earn a reputation as a live band. Indeed, they seemed so sure of themselves that half of the double-album 'Untitled' was a recording of a live performance. As if that wasn't amazing enough, the other half saw McGuinn back on form as a songwriter. He'd been commissioned, with Jaques Levy, to write a musical version of Ibsen's *Peer Gynt, Gene Tryp.* The musical fell through, but out of it came a batch of fine McGuinn/Levy songs, all of which slotted into the classic Byrds mould of weary resignation. In 'Chestnut Mare', McGuinn sings of 'Catch(ing) that horse if I can', knowing that when he does he'll lose it again, and soon. 'Just A Season' offers a bleaker and sadder version of 'Change Is Now':

'If all my days were hills to climb,
And circles without reason,
If all I was was passing time,
My life was just a reason.'

Change seemed impossible for the Byrds and, just as McGuinn's philosophy was becoming stuck in a rut, all that was

left for the group was to continue in the hope that something would turn up. In 1972, after another two albums — 'Byrdmaniax' and 'Farther Along' — McGuinn gave in and folded the Byrds to, of all things, reform the original five Byrds. The idea was to see if in an atmosphere of revived 45s, the group could take off yet again. The album, 'Byrds', was a failure: there was nothing to return to.

Solo Album

But if 'Byrds' managed to demonstrate that there wasn't any magic left in the original Byrds by 1973, it helped lay the ghost of the Byrds for McGuinn. Quickly after 'Byrds' came McGuinn's solo album, 'Roger McGuinn'. It was this album rather than 'Byrds' that was in the tradition of the Byrds: Hillman, Clarke, Crosby and even Dylan were all in there helping out as McGuinn re-worked his old themes of space, technology, and of course helpless weariness . . . but this time with a spark of optimism:

'The water is wide, I cannot cross over
And neither have I wings to fly.
Build me a boat that I can carry two
And both shall roam my love and I.'

McGuinn, one of the initiators though not always the focus of the Byrds' sound, had certainly outlasted all the other members of the group in producing their distinctive brand of music.

SONNY & CHER

In 1965, at a time when the initial impact of the Beatles, the Stones and Dylan had just passed, Sonny and Cher were quite literally a breath of fresh spring air.

Whatever direction pop had been moving in, Sonny and Cher gave it the momentum to keep moving. If pop, which was for a time exciting, fresh, spirited and colourful, seemed to be temporarily stagnating, then Sonny and Cher were the ones who pushed it back on the right road again.

'I Got You Babe' is arguably one of the finest pop songs of the '60s. As a humble three-minute pop song, with no pretensions to anything else, something which was just fulfilling commercial requirements, it was perfect. It was moulded in the electric-folk style of the time, which had become prominent with songs like the Byrds' recording of Bob Dylan's 'Mr. Tambourine Man' and many of the records by the Turtles and the Lovin' Spoonful. Further, the song latched on to the growing independence that young people were learning. They'd got each other, and that was where their moral obligations lay, and they had a right to be independent of their elders and go their own way. 'So don't let them say your hair's too long/'Cause I know with you I can't go wrong', as well as, 'They say our love won't pay the rent/'Fore it's earned, our money's all been spent'. As much as the Beatles with 'Say the word — love' on 'Rubber Soul', Sonny and Cher anticipated the summer of love, and they first personified hippie happiness.

More than their lyrics, and their evident (though carefully publicized) romantic relationship, they dressed the part — in an off-beat and individual fashion: Sonny in striped pants and fur jackets, and Cher in similar garb. There were always photographs of them arriving or departing from international airports; their youthful rebellion in matters of hair and dress placing them among the foremost representatives of the youth of that time. They were always being thrown out of fashionable restaurants and hotels because of the way they dressed.

For a time, they made even the Rolling Stones seem staid.

Also Cher herself practically set the standard for the way girls dressed, for a long time afterwards. She wore flared pants and tank-tops, and had long sleek hair parted in the middle. Half-American Indian (she had been born Cherilyn Saksian in May, 1946, in El Centro, California), she had dark, piercing good looks. In a way she was the ultimate in seductive casualness; in all respects the archetypal female hippie.

It's not surprising that Sonny and Cher were therefore very fashionable among hippie society. The Rolling Stones had slept on their floor during their first US tour; and it would always be Sonny and Cher who hosted parties for visiting hippie dignitaries.

Cher was dark, attractive, well-proportioned and 19; ideally suited to the part she was playing. Sonny however was less well-suited. For a start, he was almost 30 at that time. He'd been born Salvatore Bono on February 16th, 1935 in Detroit, the son of Italian immigrants who moved to Los Angeles after he was born. For a while he worked with his father on the assembly-line of Douglas Aircraft. By 1958, however, he found himself supporting a wife and daughter, and duly took a succession of menial jobs, such as masseur and waiter, to keep them. Then, while working as a truck driver along Sunset Strip, he was induced to go into some record offices to audition some songs he'd written. He was successful, and was given a job as apprentice producer with Specialty records.

Ambitious And Clever

Although Sonny was ambitious and clever, and even then probably had a good ear for a commercial song, he found progress difficult. He was still without a real break in the business when he got an opportunity to work with Phillies records, as assistant to no less than Phil Spector.

By this time, his marriage was in ruins, and he was dating Cher, who was still at school, though harbouring very real ambitions to become an actress. (Her mother kept taking her back to Arkansas, since she considered that Sonny and the West Coast were a very bad influence on Cher.)

Sonny and Cher had met in 1963, and then in 1964 they took a day trip to Tijuana and got married. Sonny was forever trying to get Cher a gig at the studios, but Spector never considered her as having much talent. Especially as, to begin with, she was still very young, and had a hard, untutored voice that sounded less than convincing. Sonny's solitary achievement in fact, was to get her singing back-up vocals one day at the Crystals' recording of 'Da Doo Ron Ron', when Darlene Love didn't turn up.

But Sonny wanted more personal success for himself and his new wife. So, he made use of his access to recording studios by making demos together, and finally — as Caesar and Cleo — fully-fledged records. That novelty approach didn't get them anywhere, however, so they reverted to

32

That beautiful couple, Sonny and Cher. Opp: Cher and daughter, Chastity, with matching dresses.

The informality and casualness of Sonny and Cher was always their best asset on stage.

their real names and made one record for Reprise, 'Baby Don't Go'. From there they moved to Atlantic, for whom they recorded 'Just You', another Sonny composition with unashamed romantic lyrics. The sound was definitely sub-Spector, with heavy piano accompaniment, and so after that Harold Battiste came in to do the arrangements. He suggested flutes and things, and the jingle-jangle feel that made their sound so contemporary quickly emerged. After that Sonny wrote 'I Got You Babe' . . . and soon Sonny and Cher were international celebrities.

Back then, in 1965, they were not only the voice of the young, but the image of the young. It was therefore all the more interesting that their lyrics should preach such true love. In that respect, at least Sonny was no more or less sloppily romantic than all the previous generations. But their kind of love was wild, and they certainly fulfilled the romantic aspirations of their own particular generation. Unlikely as it might seem they made love and marriage fashionable.

After 'I Got You Babe', Sonny and Cher enjoyed a stream of hit records. Sonny was a brilliant songwriter — and if that remark needs qualifying, it is only to say that he was brilliant at pastiche, picking up on other people's ideas. Most of his songs had a familiar ring about them and were borrowed from other sources. But they did have a hit formula, and together with Harold Battiste's arrangements, Cher's dark good looks and, by now, strong

vocals, they made for a very potent combination.

Whether they made records together or separately, for a golden two-year period they couldn't miss. Sonny recorded 'Laugh At Me' (an invitation which many of the older generation had no hesitation in accepting), while Cher recorded songs that Sonny had written for her, such as 'Bang Bang', as well as Bob Dylan's 'All I Really Want To Do'.

By 1967, though, their huge success began to abate. Partly this was due to the fact that Sonny was hardly flexible as a composer, and to a certain extent he'd exhausted the limitations of his style; and partly it was because they no longer seemed weird or outrageous, because by then the rest of America's youth had caught up with them. When all the couples looked like they did, there was nothing much to make them distinctive. A third reason was that 1967 saw the explosion of the whole acid rock phase, and Sonny was decidedly hard-line in his attitude towards drugs. He was quite outspoken about this, and in 1968 he and Cher even made an anti-dope movie for school-children.

· By this time Sonny and Cher had, however, already made their first feature movie together. It was called *Good Times*, and was directed by William Friedkin, who has since gained recognition as the director of *The French Connection* and *The Exorcist*. The movie was a zany look at the world of Sonny and Cher.

In the summer of 1968 they announced

from the stage of Madison Square Garden to an audience of 40,000 that they were about to become parents — showing that they were still the godparents of the children of the revolution. (Although they lost that child, they did have a daughter the next year.) From this time, however, their role began to change, partly because Sonny came to seem almost square in relation to some of the things that were happening around. In 1969 they made a second movie titled *Chastity* after the name of their daughter, but it was not successful. In any case, by now Sonny and Cher were increasingly acting out the role of the concerned parent, rather than that of the rebellious teenager. They were on the board of the Drug Abuse Council, as well as of the Cerebral Palsy Foundation. In addition, they were regularly to be found helping at benefit concerts for Democratic Party candidates such as Bobby Kennedy and Hubert Humphrey.

The Cabaret Circuit

Sonny and Cher therefore gradually elected to perform for Mom and Dad rather than for the kids. In 1970, by which time Cher had become a successful model for such magazines as *Vogue*, they opted for the Las Vegas club circuit; and then in 1971 got their own TV show — which was to run uninterrupted for two years. On the cabaret circuit, they were hugely successful, delivering middle-of-the-road fare to a new audience which found them as irresistible as the one of old. In the TV show, Cher had ample opportunities to fulfil her ambitions to be an actress, as the shows were basically light entertainment laced with comedy sketches in which they both revelled.

If there's any lesson to be learnt from all this, it's that Sonny and Cher have always demonstrated an unparalleled survival ability, right from the time in 1965 when people claimed that they were so faddish they wouldn't last more than a few hours. Remembering also that whatever field you're operating in, you're only as good as your last record, Cher's recording career has undergone a thorough revival in the '70s. In 1973 she topped the US charts with 'Half Breed', and a year before that had great success with 'Gypsies, Tramps And Thieves', a theme that in many ways typifies her whole image. Since the time of 'Little Man' and 'Bang Bang', which both employed gypsy violin, and camp-fire musical effects, Cher had been considered in that light.

Unfortunately for this story of one of showbiz's most successful marriages, they didn't live happily ever after. At least, not together. Despite the renewed success of recent years, Sonny and Cher were growing further apart and in 1975 they were divorced. Cher married Gregg Allman later in the same year.

If their best days had ended, they would at least be remembered as a team who imbued rock with a terrific sense of fun, as well as the couple who first offered a prescription for true love — hippie-style.

THE MAMAS & PAPAS

The Mamas and Papas were America's first hippie group. Refugees from an increasingly competitive New York folk-rock scene, a scene that had blossomed with the advent of Dylan and, later, the Lovin' Spoonful, they appeared in the winter of 1965 looking like Greenwich Village personified, two guys and two girls in funny hats and beatnik clothes singing about love and peace and do your own thing.

All this was after the Beatles, but before acid rock, when the attentions of American teenagers were gradually turning away from the sort of groups that Britain was sending over in the wake of the 'Beat Boom' towards newer styles of music — and culture — that were fundamentally American. Dylan himself had been mainly responsible for this, but even in 1966 he was still regarded by the teenage record buying public as primarily a folkie: his influence was on other musicians and songwriters, in pop music generally as well as on the folk scene, and so teenagers tended to get his message second-hand. They got it from groups like the Turtles, who recorded Dylan's 'It Ain't Me Babe' in 1965 to a pop backing; from the Byrds, whose synthesis of folk and pop styles was both innovatory and influential in itself; and even from Barry McGuire and Sonny and Cher, who took Dylan's message, added rock accompaniment and a Spectorish sound and called that folk-rock.

Much of this movement came from people with a view to no more than cynical exploitation of a new craze; but there were some people around whose backgrounds were in folk music, whose social and political beliefs were sincere, and whose musical ability was genuine — who would make a more lasting impression. The Mamas and Papas were such people.

Although they had, by the time of their first hit, 'California Dreamin'', settled in

Pictorial Press

Pictorial Press

The Mamas and Papas, from left to right: Denny Doherty, the late Cass Elliot, Michelle Gilliam and John Phillips.

Los Angeles, California, they had begun as a folk singing quartet in Greenwich Village, New York. John Phillips and Michelle Gilliam were man and wife, and had sung and played in various folk groups in the Village before meeting and deciding to join forces with Cass Elliott, a young college student, and her beatnik sidekick, Denny Doherty. Later, they were to tell their story in one of their biggest hits, 'Creeque Alley', which included references to John Sebastian of the Lovin' Spoonful (who had been, with Denny and Cass, a member of the Mugwumps, regarded by many as the first New York folk group of any importance), Barry McGuire and Roger McGuinn of the Byrds; all three of whom were important, though in vastly different ways, for helping to spread the word about folk-rock.

The Promised Land

Having come together, the four spent some time in the Virgin Islands perfecting their vocal style, and then migrated to the West Coast in search of work and a clear head. California was an appropriate place to migrate to: it was the home of the pop industry itself, it was warm and calm, and it was, as Chuck Berry had put it some 10 years previously, the Promised Land — where anybody could make it. In the middle of a New York winter it was the only place to set one's sights on. As Phillips wrote, in 'California Dreamin'':

36

*'I'd be safe and warm if I was in L.A.,
California dreamin' on such a winter's day'.*

Phillips had known Barry McGuire, an ex-member of the New Christy Minstrels and at the time high in the charts with 'Eve Of Destruction', from his days in Greenwich Village, and they were quick to renew their association when the Mamas and Papas finally did arrive in LA McGuire introduced Phillips to his record producer, Lou Adler, and it was really a case of Mr. Stanley meeting Dr. Livingstone, so important was their collaboration to become.

Adler had been working on the West Coast since the late '50s, and had at one time been one half of a songwriting partnership with trumpeter Herb Alpert. He had produced Jan and Dean and Sam Cooke, and had been the first producer on the West Coast to work independently of record companies — leasing his productions to different labels for distribution and promotion. In 1964 he formed his own record company, Dunhill, to provide an outlet for his work with Johnny Rivers, America's first discotheque star, and for the new 'protest' music that McGuire specialised in. In the Mamas and Papas, Adler had found exactly the kind of group he had been looking for. Taken aback a little by their mode of dress, he realised the potential novelty value of a group with such an image, but, more than this, he immediately realised the com-

mercial potential of their music.

Adler knew that 'protest' as such couldn't last, but that pop music which was positive in its attitude to life, rather than entirely negative or irrelevant, could. What was so attractive about the Mamas and Papas, apart from their image, was the message of their music. While the protesters complained about the way things were, the Mamas and Papas sang about the way things should be. Their message amounted, quite simply, to 'do your own thing', but a good two years before that phrase slipped into everyday usage:

*'You've got to go where you wanna go,
Do what you wanna do . . . '*

('Go Where You Wanna Go')

The Mamas and Papas were essentially a folk group in the style of Peter, Paul and Mary, but only John and Denny played instruments and these were never given as much emphasis, on records or in performance, as their voices. So when Adler brought the group to the recording studio he was faced with a minor problem: the image and the message were perfect, but he knew that he could not just take them into a recording studio and expect them to turn out an instant pop hit. Folk-rock may have been the new thing, but folk music alone was not a commercial proposition. Adler altered nothing; he left Phillips to work out the vocal arrangements, and the group to harmonise as they thought suitable. Vocally and visually, they remained the same.

Musical Roots

All Adler did was to bring together the same rhythm section that he had used on his records with Johnny Rivers and let them back the group on the recording sessions. The section consisted of Hal Blaine, a former show drummer for Patti Page, Larry Knechtel, later of Bread, bassist Joe Osborn and guitarist Glen Campbell — later to find fame as a singer in his own right — all of whom had their musical roots in rhythm & blues, rock & roll, and, in Campbell's case, country music. The combination produced the unique Mamas and Papas sound — Californian beat meeting Greenwich Village melody — in its own way as perfect a marriage of musical styles as the Byrds had produced with their version of Dylan's 'Mr. Tambourine Man'.

The Mamas and Papas' vocal sound was an extension to four-part harmony of the three-part harmony that trios like Peter, Paul and Mary had used, but it was far more intricate and innovative than that of folk-based groups like the British Seekers — who found success around the same time and who worked on the same musical principle. The vocal blend was in itself unique: Michelle sang soft and sweet with a clarity comparable to Joan Baez at her very best, while Cass sang in a slightly harsher tone. John and Denny shared bass and treble parts equally, sometimes allowing each other to take lead vocal.

They had a string of successes in 1966: 'Monday, Monday', 'I Saw Her Again Last Night', 'Look Through My Window', 'Words Of Love'. They made an album called 'If You Can Believe Your Eyes And Ears' which, even in its title, seemed to sum up the group's very appeal to American teenagers. Someone dubbed them 'the Royal Family of American Pop', and it was a tag they consistently lived up to. When, in the early part of 1967, attention shifted away from New York and London to the West Coast, and particularly San Franciso, the Mamas and Papas came to be seen as leaders not only of American pop music, but of the new youth culture itself. It didn't matter that the Mamas and Papas were resident in Los Angeles and not San Francisco, or that they sang folk-rock and not acid rock; it was enough that they were Californian, that they sang about love and happiness and nurtured the 'hippie' image.

In fact, the group were singing songs that expressed hippie philosophy and eulogised the hippie way of life long before even the first murmurings of flower power. This was before hippiedom found any coherent philosophical basis, and before the drug scene gained national attention. The way the Mamas and Papas sang it, teenage youth was becoming increasingly aware of its own free spirits ('Go Where You Wanna Go'), and was wishing to relieve itself of the pressures of city living

and return to a more pastoral existence ('California Dreamin'', 'Twelve Thirty'). The message was always simple and understated, and social comment or protest never once figured in their songs.

Most of the songs were written by John Phillips and Michelle Gilliam, but the group also included material by writers as diverse as Lennon and McCartney and Rodgers and Hart in their repertoire. The Rodgers and Hart songs were personal favourites of Mama Cass, and she sang them like a typical '30s trouper. As time went on, the group began to record more and more material that was fundamentally pop-based, songs like 'Twist And Shout', 'Dancing In The Street' and 'My Girl', most of which had already been hits for other artists. All this was ostensibly in an effort to show off their vocal range, but the Mamas and Papas treatments tended to add little to the original versions, and invariably sounded inferior. They slowed down 'Twist And Shout' to ballad pace and added a complex harmonic arrangement, but only succeeded in robbing the song of all its excitement.

With folk music behind them the Mamas and Papas tried to develop as a pop group, but could only end up repeating themselves. American youth still loved them, of course, and singles like 'Dedicated To The One I love' and 'Creeque Alley' could only confirm its faith in them, but musically the group did not develop in the same way that, say, their contemporaries the Lovin' Spoonful did. This was partly because they had started off so well and could only do so much before starting to fall back on what one critic called 'mannered self-imitation'; and partly because the human voice itself has limitations which, stylistically, can be prohibitive. The Mamas and Papas' true importance, in the context of the mid-'60s, lay in the life-style they popularised and the philosophy they helped to propagate.

Ceaseless Tours

So, after a while, their records began to sound bland and pedestrian, like the Ray Conniff cover versions of their songs — simple, uninspired vocal precision and very ordinary harmonies. It wasn't their fault. They were people whose only interest in the business was to make their own kind of music and please others with it. They were creative people but no geniuses, and they couldn't cope with the ceaseless tours of America and Europe and the endless demands on them to make record after record. Instead of sounding fresh and alive, as they were expected to do for as long as the public was prepared to buy their records, eventually they got to sounding stale and repetitive.

In 1968 they quarrelled and the essential harmony, personal as well as musical, that had kept them together finally broke down. In interviews, Papa John tried to explain that they had never intended to stay together long, that they were just friends who had joined forces and had rather outstayed each others'

John Phillips in the film *Monterey Pop*, which he produced with Lou Adler.

welcome. They split. Cass Elliott went solo and embarked on a successful and worthwhile career singing in cabaret, that sadly led to her death in London in the summer of 1974. Denny Doherty returned to the Village and picked up the threads of a solo career himself. He made one album that was a commercial failure, but nothing has been heard from him since. John and Michelle followed individual careers, John keeping alive his association with Lou Adler. In 1967 he and Adler had produced the anthem of flower power, 'If You're Going To San Francisco' for Scott McKenzie, but they failed to ever repeat this overwhelming international success.

In a sense, the Mamas and Papas faded out with the love scene that was so much a part of youth culture in 1967. Flower power couldn't last, autumn had to come and with it the formal burial of that love scene. The hippie district of San Francisco, Haight-Ashbury, had turned touristy and disease ridden. It was getting colder and the nights were drawing in. Acid rock took over from the Mamas and Papas' very own brand of sunshine rock. Only in 1970, after the Woodstock festival, did a new acoustic revival occur, centred on Laurel Canyon, home of Californian hipdom. Both John Phillips (nicknaming himself 'the Wolf King of LA') and Denny Doherty tried to become part of it as solo singer-songwriters, both unsuccessfully.

In 1971, the Mamas and Papas came together again to make an album called 'People Like Us' but it was a commercial and, to some extent, an artistic disaster. Phillips produced it, but the recording sessions produced new tensions and conflicts, so much so that, by all accounts, they once more parted on bad terms.

The Mamas and Papas are still remembered in the '70s, and their music has not dated. They belong to a period when love really did mean love — before the acid revolution had become one long series of bad trips.

THE doors

The Doors were by far the most commercially successful and resolutely controversial of all the West Coast underground bands of the late 1960s. More than anyone, they were responsible for taking the new underground rock to the mass overground teenage audience.

In their music and stage shows they pioneered an array of lyrical obsessions and theatrical devices whose full implications are still being explored. Arguably the most inventive and imaginative white American act since Elvis, the Doors were hailed universally as an *important* and *significant* band. And yet, within just three years, the Doors were to fall from grace. Their leader Jim Morrison would be condemned as egomaniacal, obnoxious and irrelevant by the very same underground media that had first built the myth.

The Doors' highly personal and idiosyncratic obsessions, greeted as liberating and extraordinary in the heady days of 1967, were looked on as embarrassing and excessive by late 1969. Rock had moved on, the pundits argued, and left the Doors far behind. And when Morrison died his untimely death in 1971, the tributes and obituaries seemed perfunctory.

Incredible Success

In a relatively brief spell at the top, the Doors managed to attract the hostility not only of the forces of authority and law and order, but also of the people they had once considered to be on their own side. No mean feat. How it all came about had something to do with the behaviour of Morrison and the Doors, and their reaction to sudden and astonishing success. But it had a great deal more to do with the fast-changing tides of rock fashion, shifting uneasily to leave the Doors high and dry.

The Doors got together in 1965. Jim Morrison, son of a US Admiral, late of Florida State University, drifted west to study film-making at the UCLA Film School. There he met Ray Manzarek, keyboard player in a local student band, Rick and the Ravens. Morrison was a would-be poet, played no musical instruments and had never attempted to sing. But lately, he had begun hearing strange songs inside his head. Encouraged by Manzarek, he now tried to get them down on tape, aided at first by Manzarek's brothers.

The final line-up of the band arrived when Manzarek met up with drummer John Densmore and guitarist Robbie Krieger in a meditation centre run under the auspices of the then-celebrated Maharishi Yogi (the Beatles' Sexy Sadie). Krieger was a bottle-neck player from a jug-band, Densmore had leanings towards jazz. But when the four began playing together, the Doors' unique sound would soon emerge: Morrison singing loud and furious, or soft and mysterious, Krieger's glittering melodic guitar lines meshing with Manzarek's spiralling keyboard phrases, Densmore driving it all along with his precise and powerful drumming.

The name was Morrison's idea. He got it from a line of William Blake's: 'There are things that are known and things that are unknown; in between are the doors.' That same line had been used by Aldous Huxley on the fly-leaf of *The Doors of Perception*, a book that had attained cult-status in the emergent Californian youth-culture of the mid-1960s. In that book Huxley had described his experiences under the influence of the old Mexican-Indian drug Peyote, making no secret of his belief that peyote opened the doors to new perceptions and inner discovery. In his later years, Huxley argued just as strongly for the merits of the Swiss synthetic 'psychedelic' (mind expanding) drug, LSD. Morrison was surely not unaware of the link between the name of his band and the title of Huxley's propaganda piece.

In any case, LSD – 'acid' – was then very much in the California air. It was the new all-season leisure fad, bigger than surfing had ever been. And, like the surfers before them, the acidheads now looked to rock music to provide songs for purposes of solidarity, self-celebration and recruitment: *acid rock*. The Doors, with their trippy name and trippier music, would quickly become renowned as an acid rock band, an image they hardly resisted.

Bottom Of The Bill

The Doors gigged at first in small clubs along Sunset Strip, Los Angeles, re-working rock and blues standards and developing their own material, playing bottom of the bill to established bands like Them, Love and the Seeds. During this period they didn't exactly have to fight off the recording offers. Columbia had held an option early on, but let it run out. At first too ragged for the big-time, the Doors were rapidly becoming too *heavy*. Talent scouts didn't quite know what to make of songs like 'The End', their long, semi-improvised theatrical set-piece, a tale of madness, patricide and incest:

'He took a face from the ancient gallery
  and he walked on down the hall . . .

''Father . . .''
''I want to kill you'''

Now that may have been a highly sophisticated updating of the old Greek tragedy of King Oedipus, with erudite neo-Freudian footnotes about old and cold seven-mile snakes. But it was also, in 1966, just a little *controversial*. In fact, it got them fired from their prime venue, the Whiskey-A-Gogo. Before that happened, though, Jac Holzman, president of Elektra records, happened along to the Whiskey to see his top rock band, Love. He saw the Doors playing the warm-up set, didn't much like what he saw, but was fascinated enough to keep on coming back. And finally he signed them up.

The Doors Open Out

The Doors went into the studios and came up with their first hit single, 'Break On Through (To The Other Side)' – also the first song on their album, 'The Doors'. Album and single were well-received by critics and audience as the latest sensation in acid rock. One track from the album, in particular, picked up a lot of airplay – the near seven-minute orgasm-rock epic 'Light My Fire'. Issued as an edited single, it became a US no.1. The album followed it up the charts. The Doors had arrived.

The Doors' rapid success was then based about equally on their own talents ('Light My Fire' was a magnificent rock song) and on the enthusiasm of the mass media for the band. Rock journalists of the day, underground and overground, loved the Doors for several reasons. First of all because they were bizarre, extraordinary, perhaps the biggest and most sensational thing to hit American rock since Elvis. But second, and just as important, was the fact that the Doors' leader Jim Morrison was so amazingly articulate, he practically wrote their stories for them.

''Think of us as erotic politicians,'' he was quoted in *Newsweek*. ''I'm interested in anything about revolt, disorder, chaos, especially activity that seems to have no meaning,'' he told the whole world, ''it seems to me to be the road to freedom.'' And on one level this was all very deliberate and very intelligent PR work, shamelessly manipulative of lazy, copy-hungry journalists. As Morrison explained later, ''they look for catch-phrases and quotes they can use for captions.'' Morrison gave them those catch-phrases and quotes, because he and the rest of the Doors badly wanted to sweep the press coverage and make it really big, to 'make a million dollars'. And yet, on another level, he meant every word of it.

''It is a search, an opening of doors. We're trying to break through to a clearer, purer realm'' – Morrison attempting to define the Doors' mission in life and delving into some fairly stereotyped, psychedelic, acid rock rhetoric, circa 1966–'7. And yet the Doors chose to define acid rock in a manner very much in line with their own ideas and obsessions, and very different from their San Franciscan

contemporaries and competitors.

The first hit single in many ways said it all. 'Break On Through'. The Doors' music was full of urgent, obsessive songs about the need to break on through to higher states of consciousness, fuelled by sex, drugs, violence, madness, revolution, whatever. 'To The Other Side'. Alongside these songs came a series of strange, elusive glimpses into the mysterious realms out there beyond reality:

'Take a journey to the bright midnight
End of the night, end of the night . . .
Some are born to sweet delight
Some are born to endless night . . .'

For the Doors, breaking through was always a struggle. Nothing came easy. The San Francisco acid rock bands, at their most naïve, seemed to suggest that a few hundred microgrammes of LSD would bring sunshine everywhere. For the Doors, the trip was a journey through a psychic wilderness. In a song like 'The End', there is a very precarious balance between the possibility of genuine liberation through violence and temporary madness, and the possibility of complete and final insanity.

In these songs, Morrison wasn't interested in anything as simple as happiness or universal love. He was gambling for much higher stakes, for *freedom*. Not political, but general, beginning with freedom from self-repression.

Morrison's concern with freedom, with breaking through, was widely understood as a whole generation's struggle against repressive adult authority. In fact, as it later became clear, Morrison was speaking for himself alone, his concerns only *appearing* to mirror those of his audience. His obsession with freedom came from his extensive reading of existentialist texts, of Céline, Sartre, Camus and Mailer. In these songs, Morrison took hold of all those wordy and weighty notions about strangers, outsiders, inauthenticity, being and nothingness, roads to freedom, and re-shaped them into relatively concise and accessible rock lyrics. The result, arguably, was pulp — in the sense that a song like 'End Of The Night' bears about as much relationship to its source, Louis Ferdinand Céline's novel, *Journey To The End Of The Night*, as Mickey Spillane does to Ernest Hemingway.

But if the result was pulp, it had a certain sleazy grandeur. Like the mass circulation crime magazines, Morrison's songs distilled out every ounce of sensationalist appeal from their subject matter. And they took rock songwriting into new and previously unthinkable territory. A song like 'People Are Strange', on their second album 'Strange Days', isn't especially faithful to Camus, but it is concise and understandable. The average teenage acidhead may not have known very much about being and nothingness, but he knew very well what it was like to feel 'strange'.

The music accompanying these journeys into mystery was just as concise and clear. In point of fact, it was nearly too

obvious: whispering organ and aetherial silvery guitar, straight out of the soundtracks of a hundred mystery movies, one pulp form borrowing from another Morrison and Manzarek didn't study filmmaking for nothing. But if the music was obvious, it was also exactly right. *This is mysterious*, it announced.

'Strange Days' was probably the Doors' most artistic album. The first album had some fine songs, but this one was more of a whole; running smoothly through from the stoned alienation of 'Strange Days', to the apocalyptic rage and confusion of 'When The Music's Over':

That particular song showed the Doors in near unison with their audience: it reflected the growing desperation of the youth-culture in the face of the unending Vietnam war, the ghetto riots and campus confrontations and assassinations. Above all that, it captured exactly the almost evangelical importance then attached to *the music:*

'The music is your special friend
Dance on fire as it intends
Until the end . . .'

The Doors' live appearances in this period were increasingly chaotic. Nearriots occurred in 1968 at Long Island, New York and in Phoenix, Arizona. Several songs on the Doors' next album 'Waiting For The Sun' apparently showed the group following the path set by 'When The Music's Over', moving out of the inner landscapes and acid psychodramas and into direct engagement with political concerns. 'Unknown Soldier', for example, appeared to be a straightforward protest song, and was banned as such by several radio chains. Later, Morrison denied that it was a political song and claimed 'it was about sex'.

Meanwhile, 'Five To One' appeared to opt for straightforward youth revolution:

'The old get old and the young get stronger
May take a week and it may take longer
They got the guns but we got the
*   numbers*
Gonna win, yeah, we're taking over . . .'

It's difficult to believe that Morrison meant this song to be taken literally. More probably it was designed as some kind of ritual exorcism, to make the Doors' audience at least aware of their real power. But the song was taken literally by the critics and condemned as banal and incredible — not to say incongruous, coming from a bunch of millionaire superstars.

Wounded by the criticism and controversy, and well aware that the youth revolution was going to take a whole lot longer than a week, the Doors edged back to their former role as mysterious rock shamans. Their fourth album, 'The Soft Parade', buried the politics and opted for some dazzlingly obscure song-poetry. It was already too late. The acid craze was over, and the rock audience was reorganising itself around different sensibilities: the hard rock of Led Zeppelin and their heavy metal

successors, the country rock/singer/song-writer school of Crosby, Stills, Nash and Young. The Doors were left stranded somewhere in the middle. People had stopped taking them *seriously* anymore, either as poets or politicians.

It's doubtful, in any case, that the Doors ever carried much political weight. As their career advanced and the hit singles piled up on top of one another, they found themselves playing to younger and younger audiences. Their concerts caused chaos and hysteria, undoubtedly, but it was always primarily a *sexual* hysteria, centred around the stage *persona* of Morrison, the self-proclaimed Lizard King, vamping around in his snakeskin jacket and tight leather trousers. Revolutionary hysteria hardly entered into it. Jim Morrison and the Doors were the true heirs to Elvis, and Morrison's famous indecent exposure burst in Miami, Florida, in March 1969, was one of the most memorable moments of rock & roll theatre.

Morrison later described that incident as "the culmination, in a way, of our mass performing career. Subconsciously, I think I was trying to reduce it to absurdity." He was tried on a felony charge of lewd and lascivious behaviour, plus counts of public profanity, indecent exposure and drunkenness. The case was still on appeal at the time of his death. A few weeks after the 'Miami Flash', a 'Rally for Decency' attracted a crowd of 30,000 to Miami's Orange Bowl. President Nixon sent a telegram of congratulations. It was perhaps Morrison's finest hour.

For the rock press, though, it was about the final straw. *Rolling Stone* covered the event in tones of massive sarcasm. The Boston paper *Fusion* would soon announce that 'The Doors Are Closed', accusing Morrison of narcissism, egomania and actual madness. The Doors had served

their purpose, and were to be dispensed with as decadent and redundant Los Angeles booze-hounds.

The critics, though, missed the point. In fact it had *all* been pure theatre, the whole Doors trip — the sex, the drugs, the mystery, the politics, everything. And it had always connected only *incidentally* with the needs and demands of the rock audience. Morrison was quite clear on that point.

Privileged Onlookers

Morrison probably never cared very much about the audience: they were merely privileged onlookers to his own private search for personal freedom. There are many stories of him putting on astonishing shows in almost empty clubs in the Doors' early days. He didn't, finally, *need* an audience. Certainly, he resented becoming a focus for their fantasies: "I wonder why people like to believe I'm high all the time. I guess, maybe they think someone else can take their trip for them."

Morrison's tragedy was that he began as a poet and ended up as just one more performer. And so, in time, the magic he attempted to invoke on stage degenerated into empty ritual. The music became formularised and hollow. The response of the crowd became completely predictable.

At Morrison's instigation, the Doors began to cut down on performances, finally stopping altogether. They still made albums when their contract demanded them. The last two Morrison/Doors albums, 'Morrison Hotel' and 'LA Woman' were both superb works very deliberately paced and programmed as mixtures of driving-hard rock and casual mystery. Yet it was all a little half-hearted, it never looked like trying to *break on through,* but it was fine, relaxed music . . .

perhaps the best the Doors ever made.

After recording 'LA Woman', Jim Morrison went off to Paris to write and rest and re-think his increasingly uncomfortable position as a rock superstar. He died there on July 3rd 1971, one of a long line of rock casualties of the '60s. The other members of the Doors, who had already begun rehearsing without him in anticipation of a probable split, reappeared after a decent interval as a three-piece band, augmented for touring purposes. They made two more albums, 'Other Voices' and 'Full Circle', characterised by their usual instrumental brilliance, but also by some clumsy songwriting and painfully inept singing. In July 1973, they chose to call it a day.

Jim Morrison wrote the Doors' best epitaph, and his own too: 'The Wasp (Texas Radio And The Big Beat)', his own personal tribute to rock & roll on the 'LA Woman' album:

*'I want to tell you about Texas radio and the big beat
Comes out of the Virginia swamp cool and slow
With plenty of precision, and backbeat narrow and hard to master
Some call it heavenly in its brilliance
Others, mean and rueful of the western dream . . .'*

At their best, Morrison and the Doors spoke to us in new languages — secret alphabets in which everything became possible, and most things probable. They made wholly synthetic and manipulative music, which somehow transcended its own carefully juggled elements to become genuinely moving and evocative. They took people into those strange, glittering half-worlds where the truth always floats some way out of reach.

The Doors, from L. to R.: Ray Manzarek (organ), John Densmore (drums), Robbie Krieger (guitar) and the late Jim Morrison (vocals).

CAPTAIN BEEFHEART

"You know, in America they think I'm crazy," Captain Beefheart was once quoted as saying. For a long time, though, Americans weren't alone in thinking the Captain was mad — perhaps they still aren't. Back around 1967, he always seemed to be preceded by his reputation. First it was DJ John Peel telling his audience on Radio London about the 'mad Captain' and his amazing music; then 'Safe As Milk', hitting Britain just as the pirate radio stations were killed off, seemed to confirm it.

Even the influx of 'progressive' sounds from the West Coast hadn't prepared anyone for the Captain's slightly deranged blend of hard rock and Delta blues, the surrealistic, image-strewn lyrics and way-out words. Not to mention the voice. The voice was what turned most people off — when 'Yellow Brick Road' was released as a single, one lady record reviewer was even moved to complain that she couldn't hear the words properly, and most people's reaction was equally negative.

But no one could deny that his voice had power — and with a range of seven octaves to exercise it in (against the average voice's three) he managed some pretty extraordinary things. Growling, grunting, soaring, twisting against the somewhat repressive form of the music, it contorts and stretches the words, giving them meaning and *power*.

Not surprisingly, Beefheart soon became dissatisfied with his band, who were unable — or unwilling — to go all the way with him. In any case, Ry Cooder refused to tour and left to become a session musician (he has since played with the Stones, among others, and made some exceptionally fine albums in his own right), leaving Beefheart to form a new band. This included drummer John French, guitarist Alex St. Clair Snouffer and bassist Jerry Handley from the first band, with the addition of Jeff Cotton on bottleneck guitar. Painstakingly, Beefheart set about getting them to put into music the sounds in his head.

According to the Captain, it was no easy task: "The way I did it," he recalled, "was, I went note for note with them. It was like pulling up a shirt-tail, you know, it was a really difficult thing." Worth it however. When he hit Britain with the new band for a tour of small clubs in 1968 – a move prompted by the minor cult status 'Safe As Milk' had achieved – it was obvious that he had left his first album far behind. The overall sound was freer, looser, wilder, and Beefheart was given more room to express himself. Most of the songs were new, and the audiences reacted with a mixture of delight and bewilderment as he strutted away on stage, roaring out his songs, blowing his harp, and occasionally ramming strange horns over the microphone and screaming into them.

Once again, though, the band couldn't keep up. Halfway through the tour they quit. According to Beefheart, "they went up to a certain point, and then when the money didn't keep coming they split. It's sure a shame, but I guess they got that damn ruler in there somewhere. *That old golden rule.*"

Being on his own was nothing new for the Captain, of course. When he was 13, and still called Don van Vliet, he had won a scholarship to go to Europe to study sculpture – an idea promptly vetoed by his parents. And his relations with record companies have been no happier. A&M, his first label, released a couple of obscure singles then turned down an album on the grounds that it was 'too negative'. So, after a year in retirement, the 'negative' material was released as 'Safe As Milk' by Buddha (Polydor in Britain), before some questionable dealing on the part of his producer, Bob Krasnow, resulted in 'Strictly Personal'.

The fancy production job Krasnow had done on the tapes of 'Strictly Personal' did not please Beefheart. As he said: "It was phazed and, how shall I say, butchered while we were in England. We don't use phazing at all – I don't think white noise is the answer. The music was done honestly and shines through like a diamond in the mud – you know what I mean?"

Fortunately, the 'Mirror Man' album, recorded around the same period, was later released to show what he meant. On this, the music is rougher, but more honest, and shows up the cheap effects used on 'Strictly Personal' for what they are.

The new album was, nevertheless, a triumphant step forward for the Captain's music. On the opening track, a rough blues entitled 'Ah Feel Like Ahcid', he lets it all hang out:

'One duck jumped down Lord
'N another one quackin', yeah
She got them great big brown stickin' out
Oooh big chicken legs'

Some of the songs are lost in the production, but there is the magnificent 'Trust Us' ('Let the lyin' lie/Let the dyin' die/You gotta trust us/Before you turn to dust'); another fine blues, 'Gimme Dat Harp Boy';

Joe Stevens

Above, centre: the Magic Band on stage. The Captain is on the mike, putting out that low yo-yo stuff, with Zoot Horn Rollo in the background and Rockette Morton booglarizing away in the foreground. Top left: Zoot Horn Rollo leans into one of those long, clear notes; while ex-Mother Art Tripp (Ed Marimba) hits the skins top right. Bottom left: ex-Mother Roy Estrada (Orejon) rides a bass riff; while Alex St. Claire Snouffer bowls 'em over bottom right.

and finally, 'Kandy Korn', a thundering anthem to a candy bar. The words are pretty straightforward: 'Well it looks so good, Lordy/And it tastes so good, good to eat' – but the guitars soar and intertwine, the bass and drums go through rapid gear shifts, and the Captain repeats the title over and over again – howling it and moaning it and wringing it out with his voice.

Back in Los Angeles, though, with no band, no record company and no money, things were looking bad when Beefheart chanced to meet his old school-friend, Frank Zappa. Zappa was in the process of setting up his Straight label, and soon, with a promise of complete freedom, Beefheart was recording for it.

Beefheart has since had some harsh things to say about Zappa – accusing him of stealing his music and suchlike – but the promise of absolute freedom at least was fulfilled: "Hell, man, Zappa did nothing; the boys did everything. He just crawled into the control booth and went to sleep." What they did while their 'producer' slumbered was 'Trout Mask Replica' – a record that made Beefheart an underground legend, and, for those who had ears to listen, an incredible musical experience.

The initial impression of the album is one of pure stoned weirdness (though Beefheart has stated he never uses drugs), which leaves the listener with a bewildering mixture of images – those poor Jews

44

down in Dachau blues . . . moonlight on Vermont . . . stray kids talking . . . 'A squid eating dough in a polyethylene bag is fast and bulbous' . . . laser beans . . . china pigs . . . blimps. For most people that was enough. The band were widely dismissed as freaks, an impression not dispelled by a sleeve displaying as wasted-looking a collection of individuals as could be easily imagined, and bearing the names of Zoot Horn Rollo, Antennae Jimmy Semens, the two new guitarists, The Mascara Snake, Beefheart's cousin who plays some first-time bass clarinet, and bassist/narrator Rockette Morton.

What seemed to especially dismay many people was the music's apparent lack of form; but the complex rhythms and crazy patterns of guitar and saxophone were simply a result of what Beefheart means by 'playing'. The band recorded the entire album in four hours, and Beefheart added the vocals in four and a half, without listening to what they had played. "I did it without the music. I was playing — just like the whales," he explained. "1500 feet down, these whales are singing, and there's just no way you can listen to it . . . just feel it. No special designated area, no point of interest. There is no point."

This principle is applied again on 'Lick My Decals Off, Baby', a denser and more complex album, which doesn't have the same spontaneity as 'Trout Mask Replica'. The band has a couple of new members: Ed Marimba (formerly Art Tripp), and

Winged Eel Fingerling (Elliot Ingber) of the Mothers of Invention; while Antennae Jimmy Semens has left — seemingly to go back to the desert whence he came. Perhaps it was the new musicians who made the music stiffer and more contrived — certainly he wasn't too happy with their performance on the next album, 'The Spotlight Kid'. "The band wasn't into what I wanted to do at the time. They wouldn't let me be there, you know what I mean? They failed miserably on 'Spotlight Kid'."

Whatever the Captain's reservations, though, 'Spotlight Kid' was a great leap forward in terms of general acceptance. It sold well, and a concert tour that followed was a sell-out. The music on 'The Spotlight Kid' was simpler, and closer to the blues than the two albums before it, and the words were more readily comprehensible:

'The moon was a drip on ah dark hood
'N they were drivin' around 'n around
Vital Willy told Weepin' Milly
I'm gonna booglarize you baby'

One reason for this may have been Beefheart's marriage in 1970. Since then his music has grown and mellowed, he has gained a measure of acceptance in America, done another sell-out tour of Britain, and, most importantly, he has recorded 'Clear Spot'.

With 'Clear Spot', the slow process of educating his musicians — ("To get them past the heartbeat, past the 'I' conscious-

ness, you know? That endless 'me, me, me'") has paid off. A smaller, tighter magic band, without Winged Eel Fingerling and with Orejon (Roy Estrada) on bass, put more emphasis on feeling, less on the number of notes they can get through, and achieve a wonderful fusion in the music. Beefheart was pleased: "I like 'Clear Spot' the best of all the albums I've ever done. I've finally got across what I wanted to get across."

The material for the record was all written in two and a half hours, and sprang from a desire to "state how it is between men and women." Don feels strongly about women, partly through coming to see a lot through his wife's eyes, and partly because of his own experiences as an artist. A tremendously creative person — he has a house full of poetry, paintings and novels, some of which have adorned the sleeves of his albums — his continuing frustrations over the years have given him a remarkable insight into how women often feel alienated. The songs on 'Clear Spot' are not simply love songs — though 'Her Eyes Are A Blue Million Miles' and 'Too Much Time' show a *huge* tenderness — they are an expression of the way women are abused by men, and of the inspiration they hold for him.

It would appear that the bad times are over for Captain Beefheart. He just gets happier and happier with his wife ("She's my biggest fan," he says, "and I'm hers"), an amazing lady, and his band seems to have come irrecoverably together. For his next recorded work, 'Unconditionally Guaranteed', the Captain aimed to turn on the North American sub-continent to his genius. No messing this time — he intended to 'be so commercial that people won't be able to remember what the word used to mean'. His producer on this one was Andy Di Martino, none other than the producer of the Cascades' classic 'Rhythm Of The Rain'; and you can't get much more commercial than that.

His following album, 'Bluejeans And Moonbeams', showed the Captain in fine laid-back fettle, with that mad-genius boogying power as much in evidence as ever. "Commercial? I wish people would stop using the word. If somebody'd tell me what commercial meant I'd make a lot of money."

After appearing at the Knebworth Festival in July '75, Captain Beefheart did another British tour in November with a new edition of the Magic Band (John French, Denny Wally, Bruce Fowler and Ira Ingber). The same year, after a link-up with old companion-at-arms Zappa, he released the 'Bongo Fury' album.

The Captain has lost weight. His impressive bulk has wasted away to a mere 175 pounds, he's found his 'cozmic particle', and the whales are still coming on strong. Now he's living on the beach instead of the desert, and he goes down to the ocean's edge to play to his great big friends . . . he's sure *they* listen and like it, and perhaps in the future a few more humans will tune in as well to the delights of Captain Beefheart and the Magic Band. Who knows? He's there for the taking.

"On stage, I'm Bela Lugosi but away from it I'm just good ol' Fred MacMurray."

ALICE COOPER

Without warning, an empty beer bottle comes hurtling out of the darkness, slashes through the glaring beam of the spotlight, and begins its rapid descent. With a resounding crash, the bottle misses its target, smashes into the battery of flickering footlights, and shatters into a million lethal splinters to indicate that all is not well.

'I hate ya', hollers the human missile-launcher, as with menacing glazed acid eyes, he lurches towards the stage where the rancid blood-splattered Monster is being viciously beaten-up by a gang of cheesy thugs to the sound of a savage and strangely sinister rock & roll raunch.

'I hate yer, I hate yer, I hate ya all', he continues to yell, as with the strength of a team of fresh pack-horses, he bulldozes his way through the tightly packed crowd of gawking thrill-seekers.

Only 20 feet now divides this would-be assailant from the battered object of his frenzied disgust.

Venomous abuse spills from his lips, and with one violent motion he casts aside a sobbing young girl as if she were a discarded rag doll. She falls to the ground and stays there. Her one desperate attempt to restrain this madman from attacking

47

her plastic, fantastic, make-believe lover proving to no avail. All she can do is whimper, ''I love you Alice . . . I love you Alice . . . for God's sake, somebody stop him, don't let him kill my Alice.''

Freed of his sobbing shackle, her escort reduces the crash barrier to matchwood and begins to scale the stage which is the last remaining obstacle.

The killer is now staring up into the eyes of his intended victim. But instead of fleeing for his life, this prime cut of mortuary steak falls to his knees and goads him on.

Gore And Decadence

Are we about to become eye-witness to a mindless slaying? Is the forever-damned spirit of Lee Harvey Oswald a rock & roll fan? Thankfully, we are never to find out, for the police pounce, secure the maniac in a strangle-hold, and drag him away pleading 'let me go, let me go . . . I wanna kill him . . . can't you see I gotta kill him.'

Granted a stay of execution, the victim staggers to his feet, laughs aloud, and addresses the 25,000 spectators: 'you're crazier than me, and that's what I like.'

Believe it or not, this is no cheap publicity hype, but the kind of response that inevitably took place once an Alice Cooper concert had climaxed in a finale of gore and decadence.

Any guy who intentionally cavorts around under the good old apple pie 'n' ice cream pseudonym of Alice Cooper, set himself up as Public Animal Number One by inferring that he was a stubble chinned transvestite, beer-gutted necrophiliac, satanic baby-killer and prize rock & roll freak, had just gotta be a shrewd pro. Then, when he was seen swanning around swish night-spots with the likes of Zsa Zsa Gabor, Jack Benny, Salvadore Dali and a Richard Nixon look-a-like, you just know that's where he was at.

The facts are these. Alice Cooper emerged from out of the mass media cesspit to become the Superstar of America's instantly disposable consumer culture. Sure, the silent majority of God-fearing Americans may find everything about Cooper to be totally repugnant and un-American, but then, this is the whole object of the carefully calculated exercise.

Make no mistake about it, behind that hideously smeared make-up, Alice Cooper – leader of the first post-Charles Manson nihilistic rock band – was as All-American as George Washington, the Ku Klux Klan, massage parlours, instant TV dinners, the Boston Strangler, topless bars, greasy cheeseburgers and napalm.

A grotesque graven image, who in six years flat succeeded in trampling any remaining remnants of Flower Power firmly under a tatty stacked heel, burying the spirit of Woodstock in the bottom of a stinking trash can, while callously mirroring what he considered to be the true face of America – the once beautiful – a society preoccupied with sex and violence. For love and peace substitute hate and

He was Dorian Gray branded with the mark of death and the sign of the almighty dollar on his forehead. A self-made Frankenstein's Monster, a depraved schizophrenic free of all censorship, and the most astute image-manipulating entertainer of his generation.

Though Cooper's contrived performance might have lacked the psychological plausibility to seriously erode the morals of the youth culture, it was nonetheless, far more effective in terms of stirring up public outrage and condemnation than the real-life catastrophe and carnage that invariably dominates every TV newscast.

But then Cooper was the first to confirm that it's all just a charade. ''On stage, I'm Bela Lugosi, but away from it, I'm just good ol' Fred MacMurray. Personally, I really hate the idea of death,'' he revealed, ''because I have so much fun living. Death is the only thing that I really fear, because like everyone else, I know nothing at all about it. That's why I play with death and make fun of it on stage. As far as I am concerned, it's not that our act plays on the idea that people like to see blood. We're just as human as everybody else. It's just that we like the idea of blood-lust just so long as it's us who are portraying it. We do it strictly for the audience. We're their outlet. We aren't condoning violence, we're relieving it. Just because I hack the head off a baby doll doesn't mean some kid has to run out and re-enact that situation with a real child.''

A responsibility towards one's audience is the least thing Cooper was concerned with. ''I never get repulsed by an audience's behaviour,'' he insisted. ''In fact, I often think that it's real healthy. When I'm down on my knees hacking that baby doll's head off I imagine that the girls out there, screamin' for the bits, would secretly like to change places with me. To be quite honest,'' continued the mock bi-sexual bogey man, ''I think I'm doing an artistic thing on stage . . . something that's never been done in rock until I came along. Not only am I giving them music, but also an image for them to think about.''

Patron Saint

With the second coming of rock Americana in the mid-'60s, there was a bumper sticker that circulated for a relatively short period, which announced: 'We Are The People Your Parents Warned You About'. Had it been conceived a couple of years later, it could have been utilized as the holly in Alice Cooper's Christmas crackers. For despite his admissions of innocence, in the eyes of middle-class America Alice Cooper would always be hounded as a pervert, renegade, and blatant purveyor of bad taste. He accepted this with pride and satisfaction:

''Bad taste,'' said Cooper, ''believe me, there's not such a thing nowadays as bad taste.'' Like a Vampire drawn to the warm life-giving blood of his victim, he establishes, ''I ask you, how the hell can there be such a thing as bad taste when the top

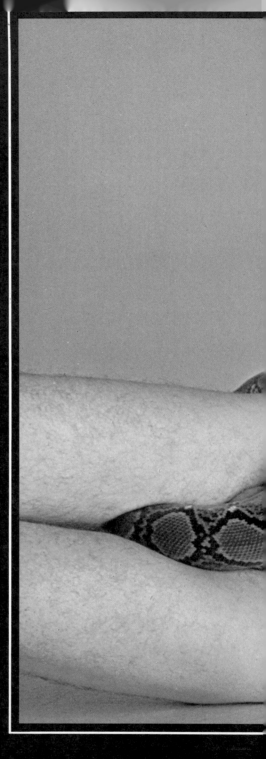

Dogs, A Clockwork Orange and Deep Throat?''

Not since the Kama Sutric pelvic thrusts of Presley and the posturing bum wiggling of rubber-lipped Jagger had any one individual managed to totally alienate his elders, win over the youth market, and blatantly rake in a few million dollars in the process.

Whether the public wish to admit it, or for that fact are aware of it, Alice Cooper became the Patron Saint of materialistic America. He showed them their worst side, rubbing their nose in it and then charging admission for the pleasure of such dubious

You can sell the public anything, and Alice Cooper was a shrewd enough cookie to realise that as long as he continued—with snake, axe, make-up, guillotines, gallows, lullabies of homicide, and the rape of both the living and the dead — to aggravate the acute paranoia rampant amongst the over-protective Mothers of America, his success was guaranteed.

The image may well have been a sick one, but one that paid off most handsomely. Perhaps the whole Alice Cooper phenomenon can be summed up by the photo on the inside sleeve of his 'Billion Dollar Babies' album, which depicts Alice and his band decked out in expensive white satin suits and wallowing in heaps of Uncle Sam's freshly-minted Greenbacks. The story that this picture tells, is that it's his money in our pockets, and he wants it back. Every cent of it.

Like virtually all of America's second generation rocksters, young Vince Furnier – the son of a Preacherman – was immediately inspired beyond belief by the Fab Four.

The year was 1964, and it took only a day or two for this bratty, skinny sophomore attending high school in Tucson, Arizona, to round up a bunch of his punko pals to terrorize the Top 40. It was his idea to form the band, so natch' he was the one who became the band's front man.

Resplendent in their bright yellow corduroy Carnaby Street-styled jackets, the Earwigs — as they called themselves — were the hit of the local Catholic Youth Club hop.

Along with acquiring Beatle caps they changed their name to the Spiders, and then after hearing a Yardbirds' record, the Nazz. They cut a couple of records, but nothing happened.

They moved to California where they starved in one room. The only gigs they could get were accompanying the fist-fights that broke out between the Blacks and the Mexicans in tatty gin-mills around LA

Vince Furnier, the astute businessman metamorphosed into Alice Cooper, gives an Olympia (the Detroit concert hall) performance in April 1975 — the *Welcome To My Nightmare* show.

Then one night out of sheer frustration Vince changed his name to Alice, applied lipstick, powder and paint to his face, and staggered on stage.

"We wanted to draw attention to ourselves," Cooper stated with almost total recall, "because we just weren't getting anywhere fast."

Breaking into a laugh, he continued, 'we had bruises all over our bodies from the foot-poles . . . that's how much promoters refused to touch us. So we decided to go on stage and do anything that we wanted. Some nights we used to stagger on stage so drunk, I'd pass out at least three times during a set. Surprise . . . surprise, people dug it and quite often they used to come along just to see what would happen to us. I'd just stand in the middle of the stage and pass right out and the crowd would cheer. The band would pick me up, I'd get back together again — take a swig of this gawdamnawful cheap Ripple wine — and crash out once again."

However, not all audiences responded so enthusiastically. At one gig, two thousand people walked out and the only person who stayed was Frank Zappa. It was Zappa's opinion that anyone who could induce such a strong audience response, be it positive or negative, must have something going for them. They signed to his Straight label, cut two albums and split. It wasn't until they cut their 'Love It To Death' album which contains their own little masterpiece 'I'm Eighteen' that people suddenly realized that they were more than some kind of boozed-up pseudo-faggy freak band with badly twisted minds. Since then they have produced a string of hit records until Alice went successfully solo in 1975.

Although the simulated sexuality in their act was never ever more than tongue-in-cheek, .they continued to upset the community.

"People are both male and female biologically," Cooper pronounced, "yet the typical male American thinks that he's all-male . . . 100%. What he's gotta realise is that he has got a female side." Because as Alice Cooper, Vince Furnier chooses to display both sides of the coin, it only adds to the confusion.

So when the last words of abuse have been screamed, the dolls hacked beyond recognition, the snakes put back in the baskets, and Cooper has paid the supreme penalty of being publicly executed, how do you expect people to react when, with a gleam in his mascaraed eye, he casually infers: "actually, there's no point whatsoever to our act."

And that's when the dollars come pouring in. It was Cooper's money in our pockets and he'd do anything you ask just to grab it back. Now that's what you could call real smart.

NILSSON

If someone had said in the '60s that you could become a rock hero without performing in public or attracting coverage from the music press, they would probably have been thought of as rather simple or naïve. With very few exceptions — and one of them is Harry Nilsson — that would have been the case. Humour, wit, warmth, pain, wisdom and a talent for both songwriting and singing are the basic ingredients of Harry's success story.

Harry Edward Nilsson III was born on June 15th, 1941, in Brooklyn, New York, and spent his early childhood in the tough neighbourhood of Bushwick. This soiled corner of the American Dream, where tariff-collecting, zip-gun-hoodlums and prostitutes were an everyday part of life, was, as Harry recalled, 'a crummy place to grow up when you're blond and white'.

By 1952 his parents had separated, and Harry travelled with his mother and sister to the greener pastures of the West Coast. For a while they lived in a trailer in Colton and San Bernadino, California: "It used to be quite frightening living in the trailer," Harry remembered, "gangs of Hells Angels

would encircle the trailer camp late at night and harass the people." Finally, though, the Nilssons set up house, and life for them became a little better. Harry then returned to the East Coast and high school at Long Island, where he showed great promise at games, winning prizes in baseball and basketball.

When he left school in June 1956, Harry hitch-hiked back to California and landed a job as an usher in a theatre, rising to the dizzy heights of assistant manager before being made redundant when the theatre closed. A seven-year job as a computer programmer in the National First Security Bank at Van Nuys came next, and although he worked at night, the hours suited him because by then he had started writing songs that he could hustle during the day.

He wrote one song for Little Richard – 'Groovy Little Suzy', and after he had sung the song to him, Richard smiled and said: "You've got a good voice for a white man, if you don't mind me saying white." . . . he didn't, and started taking his singing seriously from then on. It wasn't long before his first single, 'Donna', was released on the Mercury label under the name of Johnny Niles – "It sold about four copies," according to Harry.

Tower Records, a subsidiary of Capitol, was the next company to sign Harry. He made a few solo records and some as lead singer with the New Salvation Singers, both with little success. Then he started singing TV jingles, his original songs attracted Phil Spector, who used three of them for his artists – the Ronettes did 'Paradise' and 'Here I Sit' and the Modern Folk Quartet did 'This Could Be The Night'.

Beatle Interest

Harry finally left the bank in 1967 when he heard the Monkees' version of his 'Cuddly Toy' on the radio and both Blood Sweat and Tears and the Yardbirds recorded his songs. He signed to RCA, and later that year the album 'Pandemonium Shadow Show' was released and provoked Derek Taylor, erstwhile Beatles' press agent, to write: 'Nilsson is the best contemporary soloist in the world. He is it. He is the something the Beatles are. He is the One. That's it. Enough!'. Not surprisingly, Taylor immediately sent a pile of albums back to Britain and the late Brian Epstein.

Epstein was impressed in turn, and began negotiating a contract, but nothing came to fruition before he died. Then, when Lennon and McCartney visited the States in 1968 to promote Apple, they were asked who was their favourite American singer and group, and John replied 'Nilsson'. It was his album 'Pandemonium Shadow Show' that had really impressed John and Paul, not only as a showcase for Harry's talents as a singer/songwriter, but more importantly his technical wizardry in the studio. He had used 20 voices – all his own – with a range of about three octaves and including two, three and four-part harmonies. One of the tracks was a beautiful version of Lennon and McCartney's 'She's Leaving Home', and another produced a clever collage of at least 11 of their songs under one title, 'You Can't Do That'.

Harry's own songs were also very good lyrically, especially '1941' – into which many read an autobiographical account of Nilsson's rather sad early life:

'Well in 1941 a happy father had a son
And by 1944 the father walks right
    out the door,
And in '45 the mom and son were still
    alive
But who could tell in '46 if the two
    were to survive.'

Inserts below: (Top) Nilsson in the '70s; (Bottom) A scene from the film, *Son Of Dracula*. Centre: All-enveloping shot of Harry in his role as the son of Dracula.

Pattie

Best remembered of this album is a song that has since become a pop standard, the wistful 'Without Her':

'I spend the night in the chair,
Thinking she'll be there
But she never comes,
So I wake up and wipe the sleep from
    my eyes
And I rise
To face another day without her.'

It was with this song that Harry made an early and rare TV appearance, playing a wandering folk singer in an episode of *The Ghost Of Mrs Muir*. Harry explained: "I was advised to have a manager so that year I had one. He suggested I accepted the part. So I just went on and did what they told me. It was awful!" Since then he has never had a manager, and almost totally confines himself to the four walls of the recording studio. He has never per-

Inserts below: (Top) Nilsson in the '60s; (Bottom) The team behind 'A Touch Of Schmilsson In The Night', from left to right — Gordon Jenkins (musical director/conductor), Derek Taylor (producer), Phillip McDonald (engineer) and Harry himself.

Previously, the song had been unsuccessful when released as a single, and as a result Harry had penned 'I Guess The Lord Must Be In New York City' especially for the film, but Schlesinger insisted on his original choice. Following the success of the Jon Voight, Dustin Hoffman movie, the single eventually sold over 1,000,000 copies, and 'I Guess The Lord', his follow-up, also went on to be a hit.

The next album, 'Harry', came out to warm critical acclaim from the Los Angeles press who hailed it as a dazzling display of stylistic unity. The *Stereo Review*, a US music paper, even went as far as saying that it was America's equivalent of the Beatles' 'Sgt. Pepper'. The songs ranged from the sweet-sad 'Puppy Song' (written for Mary Hopkin and covered by David Cassidy) and the romantic 'Maybe', to the nostalgic 'Nobody Cares About The Railroad Anymore' and 'Marchin' Down Broadway' — the latter written by Harry's mother, who had also written 'Little Cowboy' from the 'Ariel Ballet' album.

After this considerable shot-in-the-arm, Harry became even more productive in 1969. He wrote the song 'I Am Waiting' for a documentary film about childbirth, *The Story Of Eric* — which gained him an Academy Award; a film score for Otto Preminger's movie *Skiddo*; the title song, 'Best Friend', for a TV series called *The Courtship of Eddie's Father*; an album of Randy Newman songs, 'Nilsson Sings Newman', and two singles, 'I'll Be Home' and 'Down To The Valley'.

A Fairy Tale

Then, in 1972, Harry suddenly found himself in the 'superstar' bracket, due partly to the full-length animated film *The Point* (first screened by BBC TV on New Year's Day 1972), for which he had written both the story and music. Primarily a fairy tale for children, but equally absorbing and enjoyable for adults, the film was narrated by Dustin Hoffman and told the tale of a boy called Oblio and his dog, Arrow, in the land of Point. The songs were just as absorbing as the tale, which was condensed and narrated by Harry on the album, and the best were undoubtedly 'Life Line', 'Me And My Arrow' and 'Think About Your Troubles':

> 'Sit beside the breakfast table
> Think about your troubles,
> Pour yourself a cup of tea
> Then think about the bubbles'

Starting at a slow pace, the lyrics revolve intricately around the journey of a teardrop, and in this delicate interweaving of images Harry puts himself into a different class from the vast majority of pop singer/songwriters.

New Year's Day 1972 saw Nilsson's second TV billing, when the BBC screened Stanley Dorfman's *Nilsson In Concert*. The film gave a taste of the Schmilsson side of Nilsson, a more earthy approach to rock than anything he had previously put on record. The album 'Nilsson Schmilsson',

formed in public, and insists that performing is a separate occupation: "I like concentrating my energies in the studio." it's the defence he feels his attitude demands.

His second album — dedicated to his grandparents who had toured Europe and America in a circus high-wire act called the Ariel Ballet at the turn of the century — secured his arrival on the music scene. Two songs from the album even went on

to earn him Gold Discs: for 'One', as a writer, and for 'Everybody's Talkin'' as a singer. Derek Taylor played the album to film director John Schlesinger at a party, and suggested that he should use the music in his films. Schlesinger took Taylor's advice and chose Harry's version of Fred Niel's song 'Everybody's Talkin'' — the only one that excluded Nilsson's credit as writer — for the main theme music of the film *Midnight Cowboy*.

released to coincide with the programme, became his biggest seller, and the single taken from it, his version of Badfinger's 'Without You', went straight to the top of the charts . . . earning him two more Gold Discs. 'Nilsson Schmilsson' was produced by Richard Perry and was the first album that Harry had cut in Britain; it was also the first time he used British musicians, studios and technicians. On it, nevertheless, much of the soft beauty of his previous albums was still to be heard, especially on tracks like 'The Moonbeam Song':

'Have you ever watched a moonbeam,
As it slid across your window pane,
Or struggled with a bit of rain
Or danced about the weather vane.'

Harry's next album, 'Son Of Schmilsson', was also produced by Richard Perry, and used such famed musicians as George Harrison and Ringo Starr. Although in many ways an extension of the previous album, the emphasis this time shifted towards novelty rather than straight rock.

Ringo's Star

About this time Harry made the film *Son Of Dracula* — the soundtrack for which was successfully released in 1974 — with Ringo, and sang on his album. In the film, which was released in '75, he plays the son of Dracula and Ringo appears as Merlin. Meanwhile, he put together another album, 'A Touch Of Schmilsson In The Night', which contained a selection of evergreen standards that Harry interpreted with both warmth and sincerity under the musical guidance of veteran arranger Gordon Jenkins and producer Derek Taylor. BBC TV cameras were there to capture the recording of this album, and the film — screened to coincide with the release date — proved to be so popular that it was re-run several weeks later.

While giving the overall impression of being a golden, sophisticated trip of nostalgia, each song on the album was nonetheless handled with characteristic delicacy, from the 1930s 'Lazy Moon' to 'As Time Goes By', from the Bogart film *Casablanca*.

For his next album 'Pussycats', produced by John Lennon, Nilsson put together a rock & roll-flavoured collection of songs, plus several of his own compositions. He followed this with 'Duit On Mon Dei' (1975), an album of pure Nilsson material in his funky 'novelty' style.

In 1976 his musical fantasy *The Point* was adapted for a stage presentation at London's Mermaid Theatre. It was enormously successful and was nominated Best Musical Of The Year. The album, too, won a Silver Disc award in the UK and one of the most popular tracks 'Me And My Arrow' was released as a single.

Early in '77 Nilsson began work on a new album consisting entirely of his own songs. In the confusing pop world of the '70s, he can be relied on to keep coming up with surprises — and very fine music — for a long time yet.

RANDY NEWMAN

In the best American tradition, Randy Newman is a humorist with serious intentions, a sort of songwriting Mark Twain who started recording his own material when he became dissatisfied at the treatment other people were giving it.

He began his career in pop music like so many others before him – Carole King, Neil Sedaka, Neil Diamond and Jim Webb included – writing teenage love songs on Tin Pan Alley. But later, among musicians, songwriters and critics, Newman came to be regarded with a reverence that few other artists could rival; and although he remained largely a cult figure, with his music an acquired taste, his influence on the music world was quite considerable.

Randy was born into a musical family – his uncles Lionel, Alfred and Emil Newman wrote movie scores for 20th Century Fox in Hollywood, and his father, though a qualified doctor, had played in his own swing band in the 1940s, Newman and his Newmaniacs. Randy studied music at University College, Los Angeles, before dropping out after refusing to take his final exams. Then, in 1964, he got a songwriting contract with Metric Music in LA, a publishing firm run Cy by Warnaker, who was the father of Lenny Waronker (who had changed his name), one of Randy's closest friends.

Pouring Out Hits

Between 1964 and 1967, Randy poured out the hits, including 'Nobody Needs Your Love' and 'Just One Smile' for Gene Pitney, 'I've Been Wrong Before' for Cilla Black and 'I Don't Want To Hear It Anymore' for P. J. Proby – all of them good quality pop songs, but offering little that was new or particularly outstanding. In 1967 Lenny Waronker began session work for Warner Brothers, producing the first albums for the company by two major San Francisco acts, the Beau Brummels and the Tikis. Naturally enough, he invited Newman along to contribute songs and arrangements. The Tikis renamed themselves Harpers Bizarre and scored a big hit with their cover version of Paul Simon's perky 'Feelin' Groovy', but the album of the same name featured Newman prominently in the role of writer and arranger.

One of the songs from that album, 'Simon Smith And His Amazing Dancing Bear', became a huge world-wide success for Alan Price, and was the first song to reflect a desire on Newman's part to write something serious and get away from the same old hack stuff about teenage romance. Yet it was also a funny song, and this was crucial. Although superficially just a jolly novelty about a boy and a bear, the song was also a wry lampoon of middle-class America.

Another song on the album, 'The Debutante's Ball', also reflected the direction that Newman's music was about to take. A wholly satirical song, it was lyrically a nod back, in both form and content, to Cole Porter, a lyricist Newman greatly admired. His target this time was high society where, as he put it, 'no-one gets stoned/'Cause it's all chaperoned'. The classic Newman style began to emerge, but it hadn't yet fully developed. There was something just *too* satirical about 'Simon Smith' and 'The Debutante's Ball', the targets appeared too easy, the satire too detached.

Never Personal

The solution, as Newman soon realized, was to take the satire one step further – to personalize it with dramatic irony. This was where Newman differed from so many of his Tin Pan Alley contemporaries who were later to emerge as singer/songwriters of worth. Never was he at any time a particularly personal writer, for while his songs certainly revealed much of his own attitude to life and left the listener in no doubt as to where *his* sympathies lay, they were never *about* himself.

His first solo album for Warner Brothers in 1968 demonstrated clearly a new development. The targets were still the same – middle American hypocrisy in its various forms – but the approach was different. 'Love Story' sounded quite inoffensive, superficially putting over the pseudo-idyllic suburban couple's view of marriage, but its real point was to expose the shallowness of such a view:

*'I'll take the train into the city every
    morning,
You may be plain but I think you're pretty
    in the morning'*

The irony of this song was that most other singers who later recorded it missed the point completely, and instead took it 'straight' – as a 'poignant, beautiful love song', to quote the singer Jack Jones. Newman himself was able to highlight the irony of the song on his own version by working as many musical jokes as possible into his arrangement – like creating a Spector-ish wall of sound solely for the chorus of 'you and me, you and me, you and me, babe', and introducing a snatch from the funeral march in the last bars.

Scorn On Sentimentality

Nevertheless, 'Love Story' was a rather heartless song, pouring scorn on sentimentality while offering only cynicism as an alternative to this glib portrayal of suburban life. It was, though, the first of what could be termed Newman's 'city' songs, marking the appearance of a new undercurrent in his work – dissatisfaction with city life and city people.

As Newman began to develop this new theme, his satire became progressively more subtle, turning away from blatant criticism towards gentle understatement and a wry, pointed irony. Sometimes his viewpoint was hardly comic at all, as in 'Cowboy', a nostalgic word-picture of the destruction of the Old West; or 'I Think It's Going To Rain Today', bitter in its appraisal of so-called 'friendship':

*'Human kindness is overflowing
And I think it's going to rain today'*

Then there was 'I Think He's Hiding', a rasping diatribe against religion dressed (again ironically) in the language of old-time revivalism.

Newman was totally committed to the craftsmanship of songwriting, rather than any abstract notion of pop lyrics as poetry. ''Pop music,'' he once said, ''is more like comic books than literature.'' Each Newman song, therefore, is a complete entity, meticulously constructed with a sense of total word economy. His most characteristic songs were American vignettes, studies in miniature that created a picture or described a situation in simple sparse language, selecting each word and each line according to its value in the end result. It was a discipline that few other writers have mastered so effectively.

In a sense, Newman belonged not so

Main pic: An early shot of Randy Newman, at work in the studio. Insert: The '70s look.

'Lover's Prayer' situation, where a psychopath finds a girl's name at random in a telephone book and phones her up to tell her of all the nasties that will befall her once he gets his hands (literally) on her:

> 'When I get my arms around you
> I'm going to rock you all night
> Gonna rock you all the day, Suzanne'

How many other writers would have dared to both write and sing this song in the first person?

But to concentrate too heavily on the sexual and psychotic nature of these twelve songs would be to miss the point. Basically the album was an exercise in black comedy, the blackness of which was given added emphasis by the nocturnal nature of the songs and Randy's own blues-inspired and negroid-style vocals. Newman would be the first to admit that he was no Caruso, but as an interpreter of his own material he remained unsurpassed. Laconic, world-weary, beaten up — his voice, as one writer once noted: 'takes on all the weaknesses, imploring tones, tight-lipped meanness, that successive songs require; when other singers try his songs they refuse to allow themselves to become quite as despicable and unsympathetic as the words require and invariably miss the point.'

Black Or White

The voice, too, was just another Newmanesque irony, in that he sang black yet sang about suburban, *white* America, something he acknowledged with delicious effrontery by including Underneath The Harlem Moon' — written in 1934 by Mack Gordon and Harry Revel — on 'Twelve Songs'. A song of awful, patronising condescension towards black Americans, it asks us to believe:

> 'It ain't no sin to laugh or grin,
> Dat's why darkies were born'

Stylistically, on 'Twelve Songs' Newman had switched his attention to folk, blues and rock elements in American music, using an appropriate style to suit the mood or lyric content of each particular song. As a result, 'Uncle Bob's Midnite Blues' was just that, with Newman's own piano as sole backing to the story of a man who believed everybody was against him — and was probably right. 'Have You Seen My Baby', by contrast, was a '50s-type Fats Domino rocker complete with rolling sax riffs, that told the story of a hung-up teenager whose girl had run off with the milkman. The girl's defence of her actions was typical of Newman's amusing and incisive way with words:

> 'She said "I can talk to strangers if I
>   want to
> Cause I'm a stranger too" '

After 'Twelve Songs' Newman finally decided to take up performing, and a 'live' album was released in mid-1971 consisting mostly of material already available on the two previous albums. The exceptions were 'Lonely At The Top', Randy's own

much to the world of pop as to the broader spectrum of popular music. His arrangements recalled influences from George Gershwin to ragtime, vaudeville and old-style Hollywood. Fascinated by indigenous American styles, on his second album Randy turned his attention to rock. 'Twelve Songs' was released in 1970, although this time there were no marvellously intricate arrangements or lush orchestrations, but just the simple, country-orientated accompaniment of some of the West Coast's best rock musicians, including Ry Cooder, Jim Gordon, Gene Parsons, Clarence White and Ron Elliott. In concept, the album was a kind of musical journey across both time and the American continent: 'My Old Kentucky Home', for instance, took the listener to the backwoods of the Appalachians — hillbilly country — where brother Gene beats his wife and kicks Mama down the stairs, Papa's blind and sister Sue is 'never let out much except at night' . . . an allusion to prostitution that would never be as funny put any other way.

On a deeper level, however, 'Twelve Songs' was an exploration of the American mind, with most of the songs set in the

twilight zones of suburban America. Not the suburbia of Mr and Mrs Jones, the typical suburban couple with two kids and a mortgage to keep, but the suburbia of the misfit, the peeping tom, the dropout, the neighbourhood drunkard. The album was curiously nocturnal in mood and feeling: in 'Let's Burn Down The Cornfield', for instance, darkness — in all its psychotic and eerie splendour — was a background to the two hooligans literally setting the night on fire.

The implication of sex was apparent throughout the album, and so rather than dwell on the theme of lost love, Newman concentrated on the inadequacies of the unsuccessful lover. 'Lover's Prayer', for instance, was the semi-droll plea of a frustrated, would-be Casanova:

> 'Don't send me nobody taking night-
>   classes
> Send me somebody to love me'

These lines showed Newman at his most typically ambiguous: must the girl not go to night-classes because she has got to have her nights free, or because she must not be too intellectual? As if in reply, 'Suzanne' was a kind of extension of the ironic comment on his lack of success: 'Listen all you fools out there/Go on and love me, I don't care', 'Last Night I Had A Dream', and the typically-titled 'Maybe I'm Doing It Wrong', an ambiguous commentary on Randy's songwriting problems that virtually brought the house down in live performances.

A year later, the release of the live album, 'Sail Away' appeared. If on 'Twelve Songs' Newman's guise had been that of the underdog, with the pervert, misfit, inadequate and paranoiac all coming under his scrutiny, then 'Sail Away' — his fourth album — found him adopting what could best be called an Olympian attitude, taking the parts of characters completely in command of themselves and their situations — in one song he even took the part of God. Musically, too, it was quite a change, a return to the styles of the first album — vaudeville, burlesque, Hollywood — and, on several tracks, to orchestration. He noted the kinds of songs the audiences reacted best to — and in particular those that raised most laughter — and began to write for his audience rather than for himself. On the whole the songs on the new album were overtly and bluntly satirical, with the religious songs, 'He Gives Us All His Love' and 'God's Song', seeming rather too glib in their dismissal of the need people have for God, whether He exists or not.

By any standards, though, 'Sail Away' was a good, listenable and stimulating album, and it contained at least one song as good as any Newman had written previously. That one was, significantly, related to a tangible situation and a recognizable character, 'Old Man'. With Dad on his deathbed, the son made no attempt to console him, reminding him that:

'You don't need anybody, nobody needs you
Don't cry, old man, don't cry
Everybody dies'

On that final line the song ended, abruptly yet succinctly, leaving the listener to consider Newman's viewpoint that there really is nothing more after death. Certainly 'Old Man' was a far more pointed statement of atheism than either of the other two songs on the album concerning the same theme. It was this spirit of fatalism that pervaded the whole album, allied to a kind of acceptance that the American dream finally *had* turned into a nightmare.

Newman's comic vision, however, remained unquestionably incisive. His great ability was always to make people laugh and think at the same time, the ability that all great humorists possess. Humour was Newman's means to an end, that end being to communicate his sense of the way things are, of the way society is, and the way people react. The 'Sail Away' album, however, made it clear that while his vision became broader, so had his humour: his subsequent albums, 'Good Old Boys' and 'K50422', both released in 1974, displayed a comic rather than a humorist flavour.

A luxurious setting of a grand piano and a young captive audience of one, sets the scene for Randy Newman's music.

CROSBY STILLS NASH & YOUNG

"Hey man, I just gotta say that you people have gotta be the strongest buncha people I ever saw. Three days man! Three days! We just love yuh, we just love yuh . . . This is our second gig. This is the second time we've ever played in front of people man! We're scared shitless!"

Thus spake Stephen Stills and David Crosby to an audience of 500,000 at Woodstock, N.Y. in the summer of 1969. For their performance, Crosby, Stills, Nash and Young received $5,000, which made them in financial terms 13th on the bill, below such people as Canned Heat, Richie Havens, Blood, Sweat and Tears and Joan Baez. Just 12 months later, CSN&Y, with two best-selling albums behind them, were drawing greater audiences and earning more money than nearly everyone else who had played at Woodstock.

They made it because they managed to capture something of the mood of young people like the Woodstock audience and the hundreds of thousands who were there in spirit. 1969–70 was a time when the earlier simplicities of 'Peace and Love' were crumbling as opposition to the war in South East Asia grew, resulting in events like the Kent State massacre, when National Guardsmen shot four student protesters. The reaction of Crosby, Stills, Nash & Young to that event was to rush out 'Ohio', an angry song of protest which reflected the feelings of a generation.

The main feature of the sound of CSN&Y was their vocal harmonies which they brought close to clear-white perfection. Principally responsible for the incredibly tight singing were Graham Nash and David Crosby, each of whom had previously been in groups particularly noted for their harmonies.

Nash, formerly leader of the Hollies, one of Britain's most consistent pop groups in the '60s with 18 consecutive Top 20 records between 1963–68, had his head turned away from straight 'pop' by the philosophies and the sounds that came out of California in the wake of flower power and all that. He began to feel constricted within the Hollies, a prisoner of his early success with simplistic pop tunes, and so set out for the West Coast to hang out with David Crosby.

After three years with the Byrds, writing songs like 'Eight Miles High', Crosby had been sacked in October 1967. The immediate reason was a political comment he had made from the stage at the Monterey Pop Festival, but for some time it had been clear that he didn't fit the image the rest of the group had created for themselves – that of a hip, progressive band, but still safe enough for the AM (Top 40) radio stations. David Crosby was too much of a hippie, too eager to propagate his new-found life-style.

Underpinning the harmonies created by Crosby and Nash was the playing and songwriting of Stephen Stills and later, Neil Young, former members of one of the most important American groups of the mid-'60s, the Buffalo Springfield. Like the Byrds and the Lovin' Spoonful, the Springfield contained musicians, who had first of all gone into the thriving folk scene of the early '60s because of the deadness of most pop music of the time, and then into rock when the Beatles showed that imaginative beat music was possible.

Stills and Young were the group's main writers, and while the former specialised in more up-tempo comments on love and life, Neil Young was the introvert of the group. Their first hit was the Steve Stills song, 'For What It's Worth', a response to the clashes between teenagers and police on Los Angeles' Sunset Strip in 1966. It started with a series of menacing guitar chords, and then came the opening lines:

'There's something happening here
What it is ain't exactly clear
There's a man with a gun over there
Telling me I've got to beware'

Young's best songs for Buffalo Springfield were mysterious evocations of states of mind, like 'Expecting To Fly' or

oblique sequences of poetic comments on the situation of the pop star, like the six-minute epic 'Broken Arrow', which fore-shadowed some of his later songs on albums like 'After The Gold Rush'.

Buffalo Springfield dissolved for two main reasons. The first was the pressure (common to all four members of CSN&Y) of working within a straight pop context when your ambitions went beyond the hit single format. The second was the heavy tension within the group between its most creative members, notably Stills and Young, who felt frustrated by having to subordinate themselves to the group identity. The same problem arose, of course, within Crosby, Stills, Nash & Young itself, and though it was ultimately responsible for their breaking up too, it also generated much of the energy that CSN&Y projected in their live concerts.

To begin with, they were a trio: Crosby, Stills & Nash. In an interview with *Rolling Stone*, David Crosby described the moment it all began:

'We started singing together and one night we were at Joni Mitchell's — Ah, there's a story. Cass (of the Mamas and Papas) was there. Stephen was there, me and Willie (Graham Nash), just us five hangin' out . . . What happened was we started singing a country song of Stephen's called 'Helplessly Hoping'. I had already worked out the third harmony and Stephen and I started singin' it. Willie looked at the rafters for about ten seconds, listened and started singin' the other part like he'd been singin' it all his life.'

Nash went back to London with the Hollies, and various contractual negotia-tions allowed him to begin recording with Crosby and Stills. Finally the three went into the studio in Los Angeles with Dallas Taylor, the drummer from Buffalo Spring-field. The result was the 'Crosby, Stills & Nash' album. Most of the instrumental work on this was done by Stills, who lived up to his nickname of 'Captain Manyhands'. Nash and Crosby strummed and sang.

Still a very attractive record, 'Crosby, Stills & Nash' was however overshadowed by the more well-known 'Deja Vu'. This album's more forceful playing and singing showed clearly the impact of Neil Young on the group. Whereas the first album was mainly acoustic with gentle harmonies and,

if at times the lyrics are overblown, there's a sense of group involvement in every track lacking in 'Deja Vu' — where each of the four does his own songs, virtually using the others as a backing group.

Several songs on 'Crosby, Stills & Nash' had the familiar Californian style of romantic autobiography: bitter-sweet in Stills' superb tour-de-force 'Suite: Judy Blue Eyes' written about Judy Collins; lazily sensual in Nash's 'Lady Of The Island'. There were also songs evoking mythologies old and new: Crosby's 'Guinnevere', and 'Wooden Ships' which came out of a long science-fiction story he and Stills had con-structed in the long, hot, Pacific summer. But most typical was Graham Nash's 'Marrakesh Express', with its evocation of the sights, smells and sounds of that hippie Shangri-La. It was the perfect laid-back song on a classic laid-back album.

The album completed, they were ready to get out on the road. Crosby and Nash were happy to play acoustic guitars and put all the weight of their performance on the singing. Stills wasn't so sure, he wanted a band that played some rock & roll. So they compromised. One half of each concert would be soft and acoustic, the other amplified with a rhythm section and rippling lead guitar.

Drive To The Sun

And so, enter Neil Young, the quiet, intense Canadian who a few years earlier had left Toronto to drive down to Los Angeles 'because that's where the sun was'. Since the break-up of Buffalo Springfield he'd made a much-acclaimed solo album, featuring more impassioned singing and biting guitar-work than he'd ever been able to do in a group format. Stills persuaded him to come to a rehearsal, and he liked what he heard. Greg Reeves was brought in to play bass, and soon after CSN&Y went out to play before live audiences.

It was the era of supergroups, but this one was a far cry from the daddy of them all, Cream. Clapton, Baker and Bruce had a well-organized, well-oiled act with nothing left to chance except the pre-planned places for improvized solos. But Crosby, Stills, Nash and Young took chances, relied on the chemistry of their relationships to spark off the highest points of their performance. Sometimes they didn't quite hit the harmon-ies, or Stills and Young would cancel each other out in frantic guitar battles. But mostly it was the way an American writer described their finale at the Big Sur Folk Festival:

'Finally they begin. Crosby is angry at the wait, and once into the song he tries to pull Young in by jamming on him but Young is still fiddling, tuning, and finally he turns his back on the whole thing, walks over to the amps, and begins re-stringing his guitar. Nash and Stills pull the song along, twisting it about until Young gets through and jumps in, licking and a-picking on his electric. The song goes on for 15 minutes, with the best electric music ever made before an audience, but the concept is nowhere, the refrain is ridiculous, 'I shot my baby — down by the river'.'

Much of the energy of those concerts is there on the live double-album 'Four-Way Street', but by the time the band went into the studio to cut 'Deja Vu' it had begun to evaporate. Nevertheless, whatever criticism could be made of the record on *musical* grounds missed the main point: 'Deja Vu', like a very few albums before it, seemed for a moment to focus the feelings of every young American who went out and bought it — feelings about what their generation was and where it might be going.

Here were songs of hope for the new life-style, like Joni Mitchell's 'Woodstock' and Nash's 'Our House', and balanced against them the powerful sadness of Young's 'Helpless' and Stills' '4 + 20'. And in a weird way David Crosby's 'Almost Cut My Hair' seemed to sum up the confusions and paranoia of living in Nixon's America.

The End Of The Road

And that was it as far as Crosby, Stills, Nash, Young, Taylor and Reeves were concerned. For contractual reasons they had to make one more tour, but their hearts weren't really in it. ''It just wasn't fun any more, what with all the bickering and fighting that went on,'' Stills told an interviewer later. Ironically, a group which had come together to escape the pressures and limitations of the successful hit singles band found in its turn just the same problems as it rocketed to stardom in the album market. And the result was the same.

CSN&Y was never intended to be a band which demanded full-time commitment from each member, though at one euphoric moment one of them was quoted as saying that he could see them cutting an album a year for the next decade. And in fact even during the unit's active life, Neil Young was working with his own band Crazy Horse, and Stephen Stills was exercising his diverse talents in preparing a solo album.

Predictably enough, since the split those two have been the most prolific in their recorded output. Graham Nash and David Crosby have each made solo albums and joint records, all of them basically stretching out the amiable talent they showed on the 'Crosby, Stills & Nash' album, but stretching it thinly. Without the abrasive qualities of Stills and Young their gentleness always seems to be on the brink of mere blandness.

Search For Direction

While Crosby and Nash have been content to stay laid-back in California, Stills and Young have, in different ways, been moving out and away in their search for the musical means to express themselves. Stephen Stills has been the more eclectic and diverse in his projects. On his more recent records he uses country music and latin rhythms, in addition to the familiar rock style he developed in Buffalo Springfield and CSN&Y.

In contrast, Neil Young has been refining his music down to its essence in a series of records which have simultaneously drawn more deeply on country music and established his as one of *the* voices of rock in the '70s. Like Rod Stewart, there is something about just the sound of his voice, apart from what he sings about, which seems to fit the times. It's a quality of anguish mixed with probing clarity, which linked to the poetic simplicity of the best of his lyrics ('Don't Let It Bring You Down', 'A Man Needs A Maid') has made him one of the most important performers around today.

Looking back, the most surprising thing about Crosby, Stills, Nash & Young was not the short space of time they stayed together, but the fact that such diverse personalities and musicians got together at all. In many ways, they were the first example of the now common phenomenon of well-known musicians getting together to play on each other's records. But unlike most of those records, at their best CSN&Y were able to spark each other

off and create a fiery unity of almost frightening intensity.

Towards the end of 1973, rumours began to circulate of the impending re-formation of CSN&Y. In the end the stories turned out to be true and an American tour followed by a few 'one-off' European concerts were scheduled for the Summer of '74.

As it turned out, the American tour and the European gigs were marked by an outstanding and most singular lack of antipathy between the two long-time sparring partners, Neil Young and Steve Stills. The Wembley concert in London, in particular, was an outstanding success for the group as a whole — an occasion notable both for the show-stealing anonymity of Neil Young and the stirring nostalgia-free reception given to the whole group.

But that was it. There was to be no re-formation of CSN&Y, only an ominous compilation album from Atlantic entitled 'So Far' released in September, 1974.

In the meantime, however, Neil Young had been busy in the studios. First there was 'Time Fades Away' released in September, 1973, followed by 'On The Beach' in July, 1974. Both showed a return to a harder, more electric sound that had been missing in his previous solo effort, 'Harvest'; and 'On The Beach' in particular was hailed by the pop press as yet another Young gem in the mould of his first album.

After two more albums, 'Tonight's The Night' and 'Zuma', he paired up with Stills again in 1976 to make a joint album called 'Long May You Run'. Another solo album, 'Chrome Dreams' followed in February '77.

Magic In The Mirror

Whatever the future for CSN&Y — and it would appear to be non-existent — they undoubtedly remain, more than anyone else, a symbol of those days of the late '60s when their singing and music mirrored a whole range of moods and reactions common to many thousands of young people. You can never recapture the magic of times past, but to have made it is surely enough.

JONI MITCHELL

Joni Mitchell, born Roberta Joan Anderson, grew up on the Canadian prairies where her father worked for a grocery chain and her mother taught school.

The family lived in several small towns dotting the oceans of wheat or snow before eventually settling in Saskatoon. There Joni spent most of her school years, displaying an early interest in painting and poetry, and being blessed with an English teacher who encouraged her in the latter pursuit.

In her teens Joni learnt to play the ukelele, and convinced a few people of her talent for singing, by playing for free in the local coffee shop. But painting was still her first love, and after finishing school she left home for art school in Calgary, at this time hoping to become a professional illustrator. She carried on singing though, this time at the Depression, Calgary's best-known coffee house.

Mariposa Festival

The first year at art school over, she went east to the annual Mariposa Folk Festival in Toronto, the biggest event of the folk year and Canada's equivalent of Newport. While there she finally made a decision to devote herself to music, and

instead of returning to college she found work as a salesgirl to earn the money for a performer's licence.

Yorkville, Toronto's Greenwich Village, was at this time bubbling over with folk talent. It was the period after Dylan's breakthrough, when folk suddenly seemed to have broken free of its traditional straight-jacket and to be talking directly about 'live' issues to its young audiences. It was somehow fitting that Toronto should have been the centre of all this, for as a city it straddles the fence between North America and Europe, more European than New York, more American than Montreal. There the essentially urban music of the mid-'60s met the Canadian cultural

63

Redferns

emphasis on nature and simplicity — the prairies came to Desolation Row.

Also in Yorkville around this time were Neil Young, David Clayton-Thomas, members of Steppenwolf, Gordon Lightfoot, Buffy St Marie, Phil Ochs and Feliciano, among others. Mostly unknown at this time, they were to form much of the Canadian invasion that had such an influence on the American and British markets of the late '60s and early '70s.

Joni played there for a time, and met the man who was to be her husband for a while, Chuck Mitchell. After a time they left for New York to play the clubs there and, gaining some recognition, they expanded their horizons and went out on the Eastern States' folk circuit. In the process the marriage broke up, pictured in one of Joni's songs as: 'I had a king . . . who carried me off to his country for marriage too soon'. In the professional sphere though, things were going well for her. She was getting radio and TV engagements and eventually found her songs being recorded by nationally-known artists like Judy Collins and Tom Rush. Elliot Roberts and Joel Dean asked to manage her, got her a Reprise recording contract, and sent her out on tour. Around this time she was introduced to Dave Crosby, then in transit from Byrds to Crosby, Stills and Nash, who offered to produce her first album. It appeared in the summer of 1968, and she's hardly looked back since.

Romantic Sadness

During the next 18 months, Joni established herself with three albums: 'Song To A Seagull', 'Clouds', and 'Ladies Of The Canyon'. All of them showcased her beautifully expressive singing, her fairly unorthodox but also unobtrusive guitar-work, and her talent for writing melodies that repaid repeated listening — even if mood-wise they perhaps lacked range, generally centering on romantic sadness.

Two main themes illuminated the songs at this point. The first was the bitterness of love's passing, and her perceptive handling of this theme was one of the main things that set her apart from the common pack. The simple chorus of 'I Had A King', for example:

'I can't go back there anymore
You know my keys don't fit the door
You know my thoughts don't fit the man
They never can, they never can . . .'

. . . puts a common situation as neatly as can be. Or from 'Both Sides Now':

'I've looked at love from both sides now
From give and take and still somehow
It's love's illusions I recall
I really don't know love at all'

The fall-out from such situations is also much in evidence. There's 'Marcie' waiting for the letter that's never going to come, there's another girl whose 'heart is full and hollow like a cactus tree, while she's so busy being free'.

Also on this side of the coin is the nightmare world depicted on 'Nathan La Franeer':

'I picked my bags up from the curb
And stumbled to the door
Another man reached out his hand
Another hand reached out for more'

This view of the world was, of course, central to the post-Dylan rock culture, but again Joni's handling of it sets her apart. She is a clever writer, but only when the cleverness serves some purpose in terms of meaning. The image, in the same song, of an 'ageing cripple selling superman balloons', is almost too clear, but the depth of implication and absurdity makes the image a powerful one.

Peace And Love Dream

The other side of the coin on the first album is a sense of wonder and exploration growing out of the 'peace and love dream'. Many of the songs simply reflect that there's so much to enjoy — from honey to salt-rusted carriages, to waking up on a Chelsea morning with the sun streaming in through the window. This vision of people sitting in rocking chairs and making pretty things may now seem rather facile, but only because its better side is now almost taken for granted. It's hard to realize how much of a breakthrough it represented at the time.

Joni's third album, 'Ladies Of The Canyon', marked a turning-point in more ways than one. Musically, like most of the folk-rooted singers, Joni was getting more adventurous. Piano now shared the spotlight with guitar as the basic instrument, but more important there was a greater 'feel' to the music, a belief that the music should be more than just a background for her singing and her lyrics. In an interview in 1971 she said: "My music is becoming more rhythmic. It's because I'm in LA and my friends are mostly rock & roll people . . . and being influenced by that rhythm . . . I've always liked it. When I was in Saskatchewan I loved to dance."

Socially, too, 1970 marked a turning-point. Joni's own song 'Woodstock' had by the time of its release been turned into irony by Altamont and the student shootings at Kent State and Jackson. The war continued in spite of the 'peace and love dream', and even in the rock business itself the contradictions were showing up rather clearly, as Joni herself saw:

'And I play if you have the money
Or if you're a friend to me
But the one-man band by the
*   quick-lunch stand*
He was playing real good for free'

All this required somewhat of a re-think of the 'dream', some inner searching to suggest any way forward that Joni could convey through her music. And yet the pressures on her were making this more and more difficult. As she said, "I was being isolated, starting to feel like a bird

in a gilded cage. I wasn't getting a chance to meet people. A certain amount of success cuts you off in a lot of ways."

So Joni announced a temporary retirement, and went off on holiday to Europe and other places, living in a cave in Greece, staying with friends in Spain, sailing from Jamaica to California in Crosby's boat, along with him and Nash. For over a year there was no record as she searched for the kind of material she wanted to write: "I want it to be brighter, to get people up, to grab people. So I'm stifling any feelings of solitude or certain moods I might ordinarily develop into a song."

'Blue', released in autumn 1971, opens with a sunny guitar strum into 'I am on a lonely road and I am travelling . . . looking for something, what can it be?' The message is clear — 'all I want our love to do is to bring out the best in me and in you too . . . oh but the jealousy, the greed, is the unravelling, and it undoes all the joy that could be'. It is the inner voyage that is invoked in 'Blue', a search into motivation, into who one really is and who one wants to be. The voyage is self-punishing in that it tells you things about yourself that it's not so easy to live with, but it's rewarding as well for what it promises in terms of change. In its theme, and the depth at which it's explored, 'Blue' stands the test of relevance to the problems of our time as few other albums of the '70s have done.

Soprano To Sexy Growl

Musically, Joni really flowers on 'Blue'; as singer, writer, and arranger of her material. The melodies are difficult at first, but so strong that they lose none of their hard-won attraction after many hearings. As a singer she really lets it go, from the purest soprano to the sexiest growl. Listening to her singing 'Blue . . . I love you' on the title track, or 'will you take me as I am?' on 'California', the effect is breathtaking, far transcending the written word, conjuring up a depth of expression that is rare. Of the instrumentation itself, various luminaries like Stephen Stills, James Taylor, and Sneaky Pete help out, creating an acoustic sound that varies from a flowing backdrop to a sound that is indeed rhythmic, bouncing along beneath Joni's pure voice.

The austere last track, 'The Last Time I Saw Richard', encapsulates the whole mood of the album. The song's 'Richard' is disillusioned, and accuses Joni of useless romanticism for pursuing a dream already lost. But it's actually *he* who falls into the cosy despair of 'staying up most nights with the TV on and the house-lights turned up bright'. Don't you see, she sings, how 'love can be so sweet'. Then, in the end, she is forced by his negation into affirming her own belief that one day she will get 'her gorgeous wings and fly away'. Despite the overall feeling of cynicism, she clearly feels the need — as James Taylor wrote — to 'believe out loud what we wish to be true'. The cynicism of the moment and the continuing search are both accepted, opposed though they may seem at any one time and impossible though the search might seem.

The advance of 'Blue' was further strengthened by her late 1972 release, 'For The Roses'. The latter is thematically an extension of the inner struggle of 'Blue', but even more than on 'Blue' the distinction between 'inner' and 'outer' realities comes to seem, as it did in Dylan's finest work, as no more than a meaningless if useful abstraction. Musically, it seems a richer album, for whereas 'Blue' left an overall 'blue' impression, 'For The Roses' dips in and out of a variety of moods without ever losing the central thread of self-realisation. Guitar and piano again share the foreground while the background is filled out with a variety of instrumentation to match or enhance the mood of the particular song. 'Cold Blue Steel And Sweet Fire', for instance, has a lovely rolling guitar strum backed by an angrily subdued electric lead and a sadly wailing sax. All that to mirror the song's landscape of helpless rage.

Perceptual Insight

The next two albums after 'Roses' were 'Court And Spark' and 'Miles Of Aisles' — the latter revealing a much funkier sound than previously, with a new Joni Mitchell band. Then followed the highly successful 'Hissing Of Summer Lawns' in December '75 and 'Hejira' in December '76. As always, these albums demonstrated Joni's ability to make you think, feel and dance all at the same time.

There are also few people who have transcended the gap between the 'urban-alienation-and-sexual-tension' syndrome and the 'sensitive-love-and-simple-pleasures' syndrome . . . Dylan may well be the only one. But the two major practitioners of these two syndromes performing/recording in the '70s — David Bowie and Joni — have both gone a long way towards such a synthesis. Just as Bowie's love songs are invaded by his 'madness', so Joni Mitchell invades the surrounding social madness with her love songs. In these ways both of them are able to link the individual and society, and thus provide a coherent world-view at all levels. If Bowie's role is the (necessary) negative one, then Joni's writing and performing represents the most positive features of the '70s rock music.

Roar Like Fire

In exploring herself and the world she lives in, and sustained by her belief in what — for lack of a better name — might be called the 'peace and love dream', Joni has helped to keep alive and well something that ought not to die. As she herself sings on 'Judgement Of The Moon And Stars':

*'You've got to shake your fists at
   lightning now
You've got to roar like forest fire
You've got to spread your light like blazes
All across the sky . . .'*

THE LOVE CROWD

'Frisco's music blossomed in the extraordinary Flowerpower summer of 1967, erupted with creativity and progressive experiment, was ablaze with the colours and sounds of psychedelia and invented Acid rock. From this amazing outpouring came some of rock's greatest bands—The Grateful Dead, Creedence Clearwater, Jefferson Airplane, and many others.

SAN FRANCISCO MUSIC

On October 16th, 1965 in San Francisco, a group of people calling themselves the Family Dogg organised a dance-concert as 'A Tribute To Doctor Strange'. Among the groups who appeared were the Great Society, the Jefferson Airplane and the Charlatans. A poster advertising the dance was designed by Marty Balin, then leader of Jefferson Airplane. A couple of months later, on December 10th, Bill Graham organised another dance-concert as a benefit for the San Francisco Mime Troupe at the Fillmore auditorium. The San Francisco dance hall scene was starting to happen.

For almost two years the scene evolved, isolated from the media until, in the middle of the 'Summer of Love' in 1967, San Francisco and psychedelic music became front page news. Suddenly, San Francisco, whose only previous musical claim to fame had been as the place where Tony Bennett left his heart, was being called 'America's Liverpool' as the Bay Area groups and the psychedelic sound stormed the nations' single and album charts. But San Francisco was more than just another Liverpool. Psychedelia was to San Francisco what Mersey Beat had been to Liverpool, but – in San Franciscan eyes at least – psychedelia entailed more than just a different kind of music. The psychedelic trappings of the scene, the drugs, the posters, the light shows and of course the music could be, (and were after 1967) reproduced anywhere. Even the attempts to change the presentation of music that San Francisco represented in its stress on community and the need for a bond between performer and audience rather than a barrier, could be duplicated elsewhere.

What made San Francisco unique was a combination of simple things, like good weather, and more complex things like the particular social mix that evolved in the Bay Area. Nonetheless, however easy it was to reproduce the trappings of the scene, the world still wanted to come and see for itself. The message, from Eric Burdon and Donovan through to Scott McKenzie and the Flowerpot Men, was 'Let's Go To San Francisco'. The Beatles had to leave Liverpool to make it big; not the San Franciscan groups – the Airplane and the Dead still live in the Bay Area – in 1966 and '67 the record companies came looking for them. More than anything it was this influx of 'foreigners' – the record companies and hippies – that ended the heyday of the San Franciscan scene. The foreigners didn't affect the weather, but they did change the San Francisco audience.

San Francisco had always been a cosmopolitan city, and as such a haven for harrassed easterners. The '50s saw a growing number of the 'Beat Generation' – Kerouac, Ginsberg, Ferlinghetti – making the city a regular port of call, and so by 1960 there was the beginnings of a beat community in the city centred around Ferlinghetti's City Lights bookshop. At the same time the students of the Bay Area's universities and colleges – especially at Berkeley just across the bay from San Francisco – were emerging from the silent '50s and beginning to object to the way their small societies were run. The high point of this limited conflict with university authorities was the Free Speech movement of 1964, but soon, with the escalation of the Vietnam War, protest spilled over into the society at large.

Unlike Los Angeles to the south, where record companies proliferated and anyone who wanted to rock & roll had an even chance of getting a record contract – San Francisco was isolated from the record industry. So if you wanted to make music you either went south or just rehearsed and rehearsed. Thus in 1965, the folk and blues groups, turned on to rock by the Beatles, Dylan and the Byrds, had no immediate access to the industry. Similarly, despite the growing numbers of students and beats, (who by 1965 had established themselves in the Haight-Ashbury district and were starting to call themselves hippies,) now interested in rock, San Francisco's fledgling groups had no audience outside that of the coffee bars.

The Family Dogg and Bill Graham rapidly changed that. At those early dances the constituents of the scene, the hippies, the students and the bands, came together for the first time and recognised themselves not as separate groups but as a community. Ralph J. Gleason's description of the Mime Troupe benefit makes clear the shared concerns of that community and its difference from the usual rock dance or concert.

'Inside a most remarkable assemblage of humanity was leaping, jumping, dancing, frigging, fragging and frugging on the dance floor to the music of the half-dozen rock bands – the Mystery Trend, the Great Society, the Jefferson Airplane, the VIPs, the Gentlemen's Band, the Warlocks and others. The costumes were free-form, Goodwill-cum-Sherwood Forest. Slim young ladies with their faces painted à la *Harper's Bazaar* in cats-and-dogs lines, granny dresses topped with

Above: Rick Griffin's poster design *Aoxomoxoa.* **Right:** The artist Griffin famous for his contributions to *Surfer Magazine* (Murf The Surf), his Avalon Ballroom posters and the legendary underground comic *ZAP.* **Left:** Quicksilver Messenger Service, who started up in San Francisco in 1965.

huge feathers, white levis with decals of mystic design; bell-bottoms split up the side. The combinations were seemingly limitless. At each end of the huge hall there was a three-foot-high sign saying 'LOVE'. Over the bar there was another saying 'NO BOOZE', while the volunteer bartenders served soft drinks. Alongside the regular bar was a series of tables selling apples . . .'

Equally significant was the fact that the dances were organised from within the community *for* the community. In January 1967, Ken Kesey publically introduced the element that was to hold the concept of the dances together: LSD. Kesey, an ex-beat living off the royalties of his best-seller novel, *One Flew Over The Cuckoo's Nest*, and leader of the Merry Pranksters, organised the Trips Festivals at which LSD, still legal then, was given out in Kool-Aid and sugar cubes to members of the audience, who were then left to 'do their thing'. The Trips Festivals, like legal LSD, didn't last long, but in many ways they set the format for the future dances. For during these festivals, the music, as often as not provided by the Warlocks, as the Grateful Dead were then called, became just part of the experience, something that in conjunction with the strobe lights and films, extended and recreated the psychedelic experience that was central to the Trips Festival. Whether or not you were given LSD you were certainly given an impression of it.

Early Dances

After the Trips Festivals the dances quickly settled down into a pattern: the Family Dogg, with Chet Helms at the wheel, organised dances at the Avalon Ballroom, and Bill Graham became full-time master of ceremonies at the Fillmore Auditorium. Their early dances were much more amateur than the later ones, when the light-shows and the posters had been fully developed. The scene was still fairly local, though by 1966 there was a vast number of groups playing at the dances. From Chicago came Paul Butterfield and Steve Miller and their blues bands, from LA came regular visits from Love and Captain Beefheart and his Magic Band, while from Texas came Janis Joplin and the Sir Douglas Quintet — 'Lawd I'm Just A Country Boy In This Great Big Freaky City' was Doug Sahm's comment on the scene. But the Majority of the groups were local: Country Joe and the Fish, Quicksilver Messenger Service, the Sons Of Champlin, Big Brother and the Holding Company, the New Delhi River Band, Frumious Bandersnatch, Notes From The Underground, etc — according to Gleason there were about 500 local bands regularly playing in the Bay Area by 1968, most of them with equally strange names. If the groups' names weren't explicit enough, the names of the light-shows and the organisations that ran the dances made clear their conception of the scene: the North American Ibex Alchemical Company, Head Lights, Holy See, Pacific Grass and

Electric (light-shows); the Northern California Psychedelic Cattleman's Association, the Love Conspiracy Commune (dance organisations).

The musical influences were mostly folk and blues, hence the large audiences for Paul Butterfield and his Chicago blues outfit, but these were always inflected with the psychedelic experience. The aim, as the title of Country Joe and the Fish's first album puts it, was to create 'Electric Music For The Mind And Body'. Though in the case of the Charlatans, the first of the San Franciscan bands to sign a record contract, it was more a matter of style than music — and it was on style that they foundered when Kama Sutra vetoed their album design and advertising material. As a result the Charlatans never issued an album, and finally folded leaving only Dan Hicks to give a flavour of the band when he went solo as Dan Hicks and His Hot Licks.

The Charlatans had nonetheless caught the interest of the record industry and later in 1966, RCA made the first big signing: the Jefferson Airplane, at the then outrageous price of $25,000. A co-operative band from the start, the Airplane was involved in every aspect of making music, from designing posters through to living together and putting on dances. On their first album, 'Jefferson Airplane Takes Off' — which featured their original girl singer, Signe Tolne — they were still very much 'Lovin' Spoonful' folksy. But when Grace Slick (from the Great Society) replaced Signe, bringing her much stronger voice, the group's sound became more flexible and experimental. 'Somebody To Love' and 'White Rabbit' quickly became San Franciscan anthems (and national chart successes), but it was the electronic experimentation in the extended instrumental passages of songs like '$\frac{3}{5}$ Of A Mile In 10 Seconds', 'Ballad Of You', and 'Me And Pooneil' on which their Bay Area reputation was built.

The Airplane managed the transition from dance hall to studio — it wasn't until much later, after Marty Balin left, that the group dropped all discipline, musical or political. But for the Grateful Dead the transition was much harder to make. The interests of Jerry Garcia ('Captain Trips'), Bob Weir, Phil Lesh, Bill Kreutzmann and 'Pigpen' McKernan were varied to say the least, encompassing jazz, jugband music and solid R&B, but on stage they were the epitome of the San Francisco sound, a band that jammed. Often their performances, and certainly their first two albums, were spotty; it wasn't until 'Live Dead' in 1970 that they produced the first in what was to be a string of masterpieces. By then the songs, 'Dark Star', 'St. Stephen' and 'The Eleven' particularly, had been perfected as set pieces for *melodic* improvisation. More than any other group,

Country Joe McDonald captured by movie maker D. A. Pennebaker at the 1967 Monterey Pop Festival along with many other '60s rock outfits.

the Dead still maintain the dance-concert vision of performance that San Francisco represented in its heyday — a vision of music in which to participate by listening or dancing.

Like the Dead, the Quicksilver Messenger Service, led by the twin guitars of Jerry Cippolina and Gary Duncan, were instrumentally orientated, though from the narrower base of Bo Diddley rhythms. 'Happy Trails', their second album, saw them at their best, not much for their 'Who Do You Love Suite' which took up the whole of side one, but for the shorter songs on which Cippolina's metallic guitar interjections over the Bo Diddley riffs created a distinctive sound. Successful though they were, Quicksilver also demonstrated what was to become a norm for San Francisco bands after 1968: first Gary Duncan left and then Cippolina folded the group to start another, Copperhead, which then immediately folded too.

Political Tone

Country Joe and the Fish were a Berkeley band. Berkeley, with its university campus and radical tradition slap bang in the middle of the town, inflected a more political tone to the general Bay Area ethos — its paper was the *Barb* as opposed to San Francisco's *Oracle*. Accordingly Country Joe's political songs, 'Superbird' and 'I-Feel-Like-I'm—Fixing-To-Die' for example, were more pointed and wittier than the Airplane's. The group seemed happier playing in Berkeley, in the park or on the campus, for *their* people, and when the first album came out Berkeley responded in kind: every shop along Telegraph Avenue, even the ice-cream parlours, had their album on sale. This directness continued through to their dope songs, 'Section 43', 'Bass Strings' and the notorious 'Acid Commercial' dealt honestly, if somewhat romantically, with dope and its effects; attempting with words and music to both comment on drug experiences and recreate the mood of them. The cover of their second album, 'Feel Like I'm Fixing To Die', which showed the members of the group dressed as, among other things, a magician, a comic bishop and a Mexican revolutionary, aptly sums up the contradictions in the band. It came as no surprise that they split up and that Country Joe returned to his past as protest folk singer.

If Country Joe and the Fish were the most reflective of the Bay Area's groups, Big Brother and the Holding Company, with Janis Joplin as the featured vocalist, were the most dramatic. Although badly recorded, their first album, 'Big Brother And The Holding Company' showed the group at its San Franciscan best — before Janis Joplin was sucked into the 'greatest white blues singer' trap that finally destroyed both the group and herself. Never really an experimental group as such, Big Brother's virtues lay more in the excitement line as Janis wailed out 'Call On Me', 'Down On Me' and 'All Is Loneliness' against the band's solid backing.

By the end of 1966, after a record

company sweep through the city, all the above-mentioned bands had secured record contracts. The next wave was after the Monterey Pop Festival, which demonstrated that a San Franciscan band could be expected to sell as many as 50,000 copies of an album in the Bay Area alone. Throughout the year the scene exploded in San Francisco. January 14th saw the 'Human Be-In', when the tribes gathered in really large numbers for the first time, as 20,000 people came together in Golden Gate Park . . . the first step on the road to Woodstock and Altamont had been taken. The free festivals continued all the year in honour of Summer Solstices, community parks and anything that was an excuse to get together. The dances continued, but not quite in the same spirit: Bill Graham was by now making more money selling the posters and postcards advertising the dances than at the dances themselves! This interest in the posters even led to an exhibition by the best-known poster artists — Rick Griffin, Stanley Mouse, Victor Moscoso, Al Kelley and Wes Wilson. Naturally it was called 'Joint Show'.

Also in 1967 came the FM revolution, when Tom Donahue, a well-known San Francisco DJ, started KMPX and quickly turned it into the most successful FM station in the States. The original underground radio station, KMPX (and later KSAN when, after a strike the whole staff of KMPZ moved there) played album tracks and tapes sent in to them by groups. It was this policy that finally gave Creedence Clearwater their first hit when KSAN played their tape of 'Suzie Q' into the charts before the record was even released. The epitome of the KMPZ operation though was its response to the release of 'Sgt. Pepper': the station just played the album over and over for a day. A similar revolution in rock journalism followed in the autumn when Jan Wenner founded *Rolling Stone*, which took for its starting point a defence — as if it was needed in 1967 — of San Francisco and what it stood for.

Hippie Paradise

But just what it did stand for was becoming increasingly obscure. 1967 saw a lot of activity in the city but, beneath the surface, things were slowing down and turning sour: Haight-Ashbury was developing from hippie paradise to a narcotics jungle, and the Fillmore was just another concert hall in Bill Graham's promotions empire. The beginning of the end came in the autumn, when the hippies staged a 'Death of the Hippies' ritual and started leaving the city for communes in the country. The scene survived on the surface; it had to — by now there was too much money invested in it. 'By the mid-'70s, rock music will be San Francisco's fourth-largest industry', prophesied the vice-president of the Bank of California. At the same time, it was becoming clear that what was good for business wasn't necessarily good for the groups: CBS, in search of success for Moby Grape, simultaneously released 5 singles and an album, and destroyed the group with its hype.

One of the last '70s outposts of the spirit of San Francisco as it was in the guns and flowers days of '67 and '68 is to be found in the person of Country Joe McDonald. Still touring to a tight schedule, still putting out albums that cut new ground, Country Joe has carried on where the rest of California and the Hippie Dream left off, somewhere around Woodstock.

Country Joe's 1973 line-up included two girls — one of them Dorothy Moskowitz, who played keyboards with United States of America. His lyrics, always biting and to the point in an American political context, have broadened in scope to include a real feeling for the game of roles that is constantly played out, on, and by the male and female in a world that seems to thrive on absurd distinction and prejudice.

New groups still appeared, like It's A Beautiful Day, Creedence Clearwater (which had been there all the time but like the Flamin' Groovies refused to play psychedelic music), Santana, etc, but they were very different from the first generation of San Franciscan groups, especially in outlook. Slowly the scene wound down and the dance halls closed until, as of the present time, San Francisco has become more of a recording centre than a performing centre. The dream was over.

Below, It's a Beautiful Day, famous for David LaFlamme who played violin.

CBS

JEFFERSON AIRPLANE

'Hey people now smile on your
  brother
Let me see you get together
Love one another right now'

The anthem of the 'love generation', 'Get Together', was a hit for the Young-bloods in the summer of 1967, just about the same time that the Beatles' 'All You Need Is Love' was released. It was the song of the moment, the expression of everything that the 'summer of love and peace' was supposed to be about. And, if there was one group who represented San Francisco, summer 1967, it was the Jefferson Airplane. It comes as no surprise that the Airplane recorded 'Get Together' for a track on their very first album, 'Jefferson Airplane Takes Off', released in August, 1966; and yet the Airplane had not written the song. It was in fact written by Chester Powers, better known as Dino Valenti, who didn't release his own album until 1968, and played along with San Francisco's Quicksilver Messenger Service from the end of 1969. Valenti is something of a strange starting point for the story of Jefferson Airplane, and yet to start with him actually makes two important things about the Airplane clear.

Like Valenti, the Airplane's roots are in the mid-'60s revival of folk and folk-style music; and their declared aim was to develop a style they called 'folk rock'. Secondly, the Airplane and the whole San Francisco scene, which included Valenti, were connected by almost familial ties. It

is impossible to talk about one San Francisco performer, promoter or manager without bringing in most of the other local figures in the music scene.

In March, 1965, Dylan's electric (in all senses of the word) 'Bringing It All Back Home' was released, and the idea of electrified 'folk' music took root and blos-somed with the Byrds' version of Dylan's 'Mr Tambourine Man'.

The Byrds originally came from Los Angeles, and their sound was typical of the place — disciplined yet relaxed, so that the instruments were all clear and distinct, like the geography and architecture of the city. Even before the Byrds had started as a group, though, the connections between L A and 'Frisco were being made. David Crosby, for example, would often play (folk) on the same bill as Valenti when both were itinerant musicians. Paul Kantner, Airplane guitarist and songwriter, met Crosby in L A, and the two of them, along with David Freiberg, lived together in Venice, California, when they were all try-ing to make a living out of coffee-house performances. Freiberg was a founder member of Quicksilver, and joined the Airplane around the beginning of 1972 after an enforced absence from Quicksilver due to a drugs charge.

It has often been said that the Airplane was the first San Francisco group. 'Only the Charlatans and Mystery Trend pre-date them', according to one writer. Whether or not they were the *first*, though, is not important. What is important is that the Airplane 'was the first of the big San

Francisco bands *to make it*, the first to snap up a big contract, the first to get big national promotion, the first with a big national hit . . .', as Lillian Roxon put it. In 1966, the Airplane signed a contract with RCA Victor guaranteeing them a $20,000 advance.

Marty Balin was the group's founder. He was born Martyn Jerel Buchwald, the son of a lithographer and himself a designer and painter. In 1964, Balin was with a folk group called the Town Criers. He saw the Beatles on the *Ed Sullivan Show* in February of that year and decided, there and then, to get 'involved with the rock & roll thing'. Previously he had met Dylan in New York, and when Dylan 'started getting popular and the Byrds went to L A and started . . . the folk rock line', Balin decided to go to San Francisco and start a group there. He didn't exactly audition people, but got the band together through asking friends.

After Kantner left the Los Angeles area he moved to San Jose. By then he'd listened to the Beatles and started playing around casually with Roger McGuinn and stated: "The Byrds were the first American group that really turned me on." In San Jose he played and helped run a folk club. In Santa Cruz he lived in a proto-type commune and met Jorma Kaukonen — still at college in Santa Clara — who became the Airplane's lead guitarist. When Kantner eventually returned home to San Francisco, he began playing at the Drinking Gourd, a local folk club. It was here that Marty Balin met him, after a fruitless search for musicians to build up the group. Balin describes his intuitive recognition that Kantner, with ''a 12-string and a banjo, and . . . hair down to here and an old cap,'' was the man for the group: ''I had never heard of him, but I *knew* he was good.''

Kaukonen joined as a favour to Kantner – he was, at the time, 'a Bay Area folk figure'. Among the people Kaukonen had already played with was Janis Joplin, and it was the strength of Janis' vocals that made him buy his first electric guitar: ''. . . she was so loud it was just impossible for an acoustic guitar player to compete with her.'' While at school in Washington, Kaukonen had also played casually with Jack Casady. It was through that connection that Casady came to San Francisco to play bass with the newly formed Airplane.

Musical Centre

In the spring of 1965, Marty Balin took over the Matrix club. The Matrix had been a folk and jazz club under the name of the Honeybucket. Balin had the idea of turning it from a quiet, almost underground club, into a centre of musical activity in the town. He decorated the place, put in a stage, and – in August, 1965 – the Airplane opened there as a semi-resident group. The two members, apart from Balin, Kantner, Kaukonen and Casady, were the girl singer Signe Tolne Anderson, and Skip Spence on drums. Interestingly, at the time Balin caught Spence, he was on his way to audition for the Quicksilver people, who were also starting their band. Skip Spence had never played drums before, and pretty soon after the first album had been recorded in the early autumn of 1966, he left, to eventually form another San Francisco group, Moby Grape, with whom he sang and played guitar. Spence was replaced by Spencer Dryden, an experienced jazz drummer; and it was Kaukonen, Casady and Dryden who provided the essentials of the Airplane's musical excitement during their best period.

Signe Anderson also left after the first album due to pregnancy and Casady recruited a girl singer to replace her from a group that had started in the Airplane's wake. She was called Grace Slick, and the group she had formed with her husband and brother-in-law was called the Great Society. Her voice, much more raucous and rough than Signe Anderson's, was the perfect complement to Balin's sweetness. She also happened to bring with her the two songs which were to become the Airplane's only two real hit singles: 'Somebody To Love' and 'White Rabbit'.

By the time of 'Take Off', the Airplane had already changed direction considerably. The changes in personnel had something to do with it, but perhaps the two most important factors were acid and amplification. Grace Slick brought with her a harsher vocal style, but she also brought a drug song ('White Rabbit'). The lyric field open to rock had been started by Dylan and his successors, but the particular

concern with psychedelia and 'mind expanding' drugs was almost completely restricted to San Francisco in those early days. Even the Berkeley groups from across the Bay, like Country Joe and the Fish, were involved in it – whereas their previous involvement with music had always been far more overtly political.

In November, 1965, yet another California group with a folk-singing background became involved with the 'Acid Set' – a group of people focused on ex-beatnik Ken Kesey and his Merry Pranksters, and Augustus Owsley III, who made LSD in his house in Watts, Los Angeles. They were the Warlocks, who became the Grateful Dead around February, 1966. Kesey and Owsley held what they described as 'Acid Tests' around the beginning of 1966, and the Dead provided the music. In June, 1966, the Dead moved to San Francisco, and LSD began to hit the Bay Area in a big way – furthered by the rapidly growing number of large dance/concert halls that were springing up all over the city. The Airplane, the Marbles, the Great Society and the Charlatans played at the first of these to be organized in San Francisco. It was held at the Longshoreman's Hall on October 16th, 1965. The promoters were the original Family Dog – a group of young people who were probably the first hippie communards. Marty Balin designed the posters, and the Airplane topped the bill.

The unexpected popularity of that event led others like Bill Graham and Chet Helms to organize follow-ups. Light-shows and gaudy clothes blossomed; people came in their thousands to celebrate and to dance, or simply to observe. The Fillmore Auditorium and the Avalon Ballroom became Meccas for the young people of San Francisco, goldmines for the owners and promoters . . . and potential threats to the moral order for the police. Jefferson Airplane were usually there, the doyens of San Francisco's own music; and as the audiences got larger and more eager to dance, through acid or simple excitement, the need for more and more amplification and more and more free expression in the music increased.

The Airplane's early sound was dominated by Marty Balin. His voice was smooth and rich, his songs mainly love songs. Signe Anderson had merely supplemented him, but Grace Slick began to complement him. Eventually, Marty Balin gave up playing guitar, and Grace Slick, who had come in on keyboards and recorder, gave up her instruments. The amplified guitars took over, especially Kaukonen's beautifully clear and aggressive playing, and a vocal style depending on anything from two to four-part harmony developed – Balin usually singing on top with Slick cutting through like a flint wheel. The folksy, acoustic sound began to give way to a harsher, electric and freer approach. This trend can be detected on 'Surrealistic Pillow', their second album, which, although containing two of Balin's finest love songs, 'Today' and 'Comin' Back To Me', also has the more energetic 'Some-

body To Love' (by Grace's husband Jerry), Balin's angry '⅗ Of A Mile In 10 Seconds', and 'White Rabbit' (on the American version of the album only – the British version is a combination of the first two American albums).

The Airplane's music began to reflect the functions it performed. Very often it was simply a question of stance-taking. But outrageousness for its own sake fitted in well with the newly awakening hippie consciousness. Like their name (from an imaginary blues singer, 'Blind Jefferson Airplane'), much of what they did was, at worst, a joke and, at best, simply a response to the question 'Why not?'. 'Crown Of Creation', their fourth album, had Paul Kantner stealing the lyrics of the title song almost verbatim from John Wyndham's *The Chrysalids*: 'The Old People are determined still that there is a final form to defend: soon they will attain the stability they strive for, in the only form it is granted – a place among the fossils'.

Love too became a stance, and on '⅗ Of A Mile In 10 Seconds', Balin points forward to the political stance he and Kantner would later take on 'Volunteers'. He writes: 'Do away with people frowning on my precious prayer/Do away with people laughing at my hair'. The huge Fillmore and Avalon dances, the almost instantaneous creation of a hippie lifestyle born largely of young dropouts, brought people suddenly together in shared experiences in which music played an important part. The music and its free-form dance approach became a major way in which people identified each other as belonging to their group. It is not surprising that some sort of political statement eventually grew out of it, and it is equally clear why it was later abandoned to things like Kantner's private science-fiction fantasies.

Mirrored Feelings

The Airplane quickly became reflectors of the feelings and ideas of their audiences. Kantner even admits this to be the case when questioned about his earlier political views: ''It's like I'm a sort of news man. Like you, I write down what I see happening, but I don't have a paper. I use my songs as the vehicle. Everything that was in 'Volunteers' has happened, and is happening right now. I just saw it and wrote it down.'' The Airplane's politics, in other words, were just a reflection of the state of their audiences. And they were as short-lived and as superficial as most writers have observed, simply because the hippie rebellion itself was involved with superficiality.

An Airplane concert was certainly an experience not to be missed. Between August and September, 1968, they were in Britain to do the Isle of Wight festival, a free concert and two gigs at the Roundhouse – London's answer to the Avalon Ballroom. By this time they had a huge underground following on both sides of the Atlantic. They released plenty of singles,

but they never were a singles band. Only 'White Rabbit' and 'Somebody To Love' approached the kind of success most bands had previously been interested in. 'White Rabbit' reached no. 8 in the *Billboard* charts, and 'Somebody To Love' went up to no. 5.

In comparison to the success of 'Somebody To Love', which got to no. 22 in the *Cash Box* listing of top singles for 1967, nothing else the Airplane did in America and nothing they did in Britain had any impact. Yet their draw as a live band, and, to a lesser extent, their album sales, were remarkable. They made greater and more exciting use of light-shows than anyone around at the time, and would drift off into lengthy and meandering jams — very appropriate for the psychedelic mood of the moment. When they wanted to they could still be tight and heavy, but their involvement with acid and electronics made that less and less likely. These changes showed up on record too. 'After Bathing At Baxters', released in January, 1968, was recorded after the group's first big American tour. Balin, who couldn't write on tour, figures less on it than on any previous album, and it also features a nine-minute instrumental jam between Kaukonen and Casady called 'Spare Chaynge'.

The light-shows and the group's developing musical style were obviously attempts to superficially re-create the drug experience. But drugs changed perception rather than the reality underlying it, and psychedelic music and its off-

shoots — light-shows and hippie dress — now appear as attempts to change certain objects of perception. The hippie rebellion was superficial, in this sense. The hippies only attacked certain areas of the cultural ways of expression — they dressed differently, looked different and spoke differently . . . but underneath, little had changed. Bill Graham, who used to manage the Airplane, was the first and most successful entrepreneur of the hippie world. He ran the biggest dances, managed groups and started a record label. He kept a careful watch on his world — he was involved with 'people dancing and having fun, that's all'. And, of course, making money. His comments to a young kid trying to get into the Fillmore for nothing sum up that whole side of things: ''Forget love,'' he is reported to have said, ''get in line!''

Water Brothers

The cult book of the time was Robert Heinlein's science-fiction fantasy *Stranger In A Strange Land,* about a Mars-born Earthman who brings with him from Mars to Earth a whole new code of morals and the beginnings of a new religion. Mars compares well with Southern California. The Martian culture values water above all else, because, like Southern California, it is a desert world. The highest compliment is to call someone a 'water brother', and the hero of the novel lives with two women in a happy threesome. He makes his appearance in David Crosby's song

'Triad' on 'Crown Of Creation':

> *'If you're crazy too*
> *I don't really see*
> *Why can't we go on as three'.*

It was a very gentle rebellion. In contrast to the Doors — an L A group who shared the bill with the Airplane at their London Roundhouse gig — the Airplane only challenged society by default. Where the Doors demanded, 'We want the world, and we want it now!', the Airplane merely suggested, 'We can be together'. At their most extreme — as with Marty Balin's last work on an Airplane album, 'Volunteers' — they came out with: 'Got to revolution, Got a revolution'. In a confused way they expressed the idea that the revolution was already here: 'We are outlaws in the eyes of America' (from 'We Can Be Together' on 'Volunteers'); but they never really knew what they wanted . . . if they wanted anything at all. In that same song Grace Slick shouted 'Up against the wall', only to follow immediately with 'Tear down the wall'. No one ever knew what the wall was really for.

The Airplane, though, moved from success to success. Only Marty Balin seemed disaffected. He clearly didn't enjoy touring, and he wrote less and less. Kantner, who used to be Balin's co-writer, fell in with Grace Slick, and Kaukonen and Casady spent more time playing together. The group began to be dominated by Slick's harsh and meandering vocal style. The

Top insert: Pictorial Press. Bottom insert: L.F.I.

Against a background of the Jefferson Airplane group are pinpointed — Bottom L.H. insert: Papa John Creach on fiddle. Top L.H. inse

Airplane had quickly become a lead-guitar based group, and that set them apart from the British-style rhythm-oriented bands. But it also meant that they became undisciplined and undirected. They lost their inherent sense of structure, and when Grace Slick began to dominate the group, their artistic decline became inevitable. Slick's voice has been described as 'I-am-a-background-instrument' in style, and her biggest contribution to the group was when she complemented Balin. Undoubtedly Grace has a way of moving, seemingly

without direction, sliding from phrase to phrase without giving the feeling of getting anywhere, but this is precisely what destroyed the Airplane. Not only her voice, but her lyrics too, shift from phrase to phrase without any overall sense. On 'Long John Silver', their eighth album as the Jefferson Airplane, she was able to write:

'You can't fly — human master
You can't fly — by yourself
You can't fly — dying master
Without a rifle on your shelf'.

The comparison between Slick's style and the light-shows they used is irresistible. The almost formless meanderings are fine for a light-show, but are a hopeless basis on which to build a growing, progressing music.

Between 'Volunteers' and 'Park', nearly two years elapsed without a single original Jefferson Airplane album. When Balin left in the summer of 1971, the group seemed to fall apart. They moved out of their communal house, set up their own label, Grunt, on a very good manufac-

Top insert: L.F.I. Bottom insert: Pictorial Press.

…race Slick and Paul Kantner in concert. Centre insert: Grace Slick. Top R.H. insert: Paul Kantner, guitarist and science fiction addict.

turing and distribution deal with RCA, and each seemed to go their own way. Kantner and Slick had a child, who was to be named 'God' but got off with 'China', and Kantner — in the face of the failure of the hippie rebellion to actually change anything — went off into a fantasy world of giant starships, which he and David Crosby would pilot in a bid to escape the strife-torn planet Earth.

Balin ended up producing and singing with a Bay Area group called Grootna, and has since moved on to another called

Bodacious D. F. Kaukonen and Casady started Hot Tuna which was a part-time acoustic band. It later acquired additional members and made several albums. Joey Covington — Hot Tuna's first drummer — joined the Airplane when Dryden left, eventually to join the New Riders of the Purple Sage. He left to join Kaukonen's brother's group in 1972, and was replaced by John Barbata, from the Turtles and ex-CSN & Y session drummer. Covington brought old, black, fiddle player, Papa John Creach, into the fold, and all of them

— Creach included — have made individual solo albums.

In 1974 Marty Balin returned to the now metamorphosed Jefferson Starship, giving the band a new purpose which showed in the music on their next albums 'Red Octopus' and 'Spitfire'. The line-up still included the core of the original Airplane — Grace Slick (now married to Skip Johnson) and Paul Kantner. Although the Airplane belonged to a particular era whose hopes and dreams have since disappeared, the Starship continues to fly high.

79

GRATEFUL DEAD

The Grateful Dead have been all things to all men. Particularly since the beginning of the '70s they have often appeared to be a giant psychedelic hangover, a crazy bunch of hippie archetypes resplendent in tie-dyed T-shirts and patched denims.

From 1966, right through the midday sun of the San Francisco flower power era, this image was a pretty accurate reflection of the band's life-style, and it became a difficult one to alter, short of wearing tinsel in their hair, performing onstage contortions, or pandering to the potential blood-lust of an audience weaned on TV violence and television suppers.

In 1972 — by which time the band had a huge international following — they appeared on stage in Portland one night in sharp suits: cowboy-styled jackets emblazoned with rhinestone-studded marijuana leaves. Their audience, of course, was resplendent in tie-dyes and denim. Huuuhhhh?

The Dead's sets have always been notably long. Three or four times longer than most; and four hours is a long time to stand up and give out all the energy you've got. For those who have never experienced a gig like that, it sounds outrageous, long enough to drive an audience out, or to sleep. There are those who have seen the band and would agree. But there are others who maintain that a musical high with the Grateful Dead at the controls is an experience bordering on ecstasy, unrepeatable and unforgettable, and sustained in a manner that no other rock band could hope to equal in a million years.

During their mammoth 1972 European tour, for instance, the Dead played a set at the Bickershaw Festival in the North of England. The festival was held in a field on the outskirts of a depressing mining town, and by the evening of the first day the audience was floundering morosely in a sea of mud. As soon as the Dead took the stage, however, the mood changed and the audience's spirits rose to meet them.

But are the Dead even a rock band? At different times, on stage and on record, they have appeared more as pioneers of electronic weirdness, calculated to confuse, enlighten and amuse the assumed active consciousness of their listener. Despite this, five minutes later they may come up with a folksy little song like 'Casey Jones', a love song like 'Sugar Magnolia', or a typically punk-rock slider like 'Not Fade Away' or 'Good Lovin'. So, where exactly do they stand? Where is the root of this variety?

For all their lengthy fedback strangeness, and their seemingly stoned indulgence, the Dead nonetheless seem to have evolved into a highly respected unit of musicians, whether working together, or with a wide variety of others. Jerry Garcia's guitar and steel guitar was prominent on at least 20 albums recorded on the West Coast, on many occasions in the company of bassist Phil Lesh, and occasionally 'Drummer Bill' Kreutzmann. Several of the Dead's albums also reached Gold status, and the group enjoys the dubious distinction of being the most frequently bootlegged band in existence. Finally, they set up their own publishing company, record company and distribution set-up, an equipment and instrument workshop, and were the guiding force behind a large number of interrelated schemes: recording studios, design studios and spin-off groups. The Grateful Dead family in the '70s reached the point of becoming a gargantuan self-propelled creative unit, responsible only to itself, both working and playing together, and treating the two as one.

All this happened slowly, even ponderously, and the story goes back well beyond the birth of the mythical hippie monster of yore, back to a few years after Garcia obtained his first guitar and amplifier for his 15th birthday on August 1st, 1957.

Jerry Garcia is the obvious uncle-figure within the complex Grateful Dead animal. A warm, talkative barrel of ten

Below. The Grateful Dead in action, from left to right: Ron 'Pigpen' McKernan on organ, Jerry Garcia and Bob 'Ace' Weir on guitar,

fingered energy, somewhat owl-like behind his gold-rimmed glasses, he has always been stuck with a 'Mr Goodvibes' tag. And deservedly so: a cross between Mr Natural and Robert Crumb's Doo-Dah Man, the Keep On Truckin' caricature. Make no mistake, these qualities are very real, and totally endemic to the feel of the Grateful Dead, to their music, their ambiance, and — as a result — to their followers and those influenced by them.

Two years after getting that first guitar, Garcia joined the army as an excuse to get out of school. He lasted nine months, and afterwards fell into the nomadic, drifting world which was the West Coast beat zone. He met up with Bob Hunter, also just out of the army, and another guitar-picker. They started to play the bars and clubs together, singing folk songs. This music slowly evolved into a more purist approach to blues and authentic country music.

In the same area as Garcia and Hunter, playing the same type of material at the same time, were also people like Pete Stampfel, Nick Gravenites, David Frieberg, Paul Kantner, Jorma Kaukonen, and a stray young chick from Texas, Janis Joplin. Many of them, including Hunter and Garcia, were working towards a type of music that appealed on an intellectual level, and was constantly open to change as a result of external or internal forces. Those forces were primarily felt at the Palo Alto Peace Centre, a loose socio-political meeting-point where rich drop-out kids hung about with artists and musicians, went to Ken Kesey's parties, and smoked dope.

Into this scene flitted Phil Lesh, a classically-trained jazz trumpeter, Bob Weir, a 15-year-old more interested in his guitar than his parents' money, and Ron McKernan (later called Pigpen), a scruffy street-kid raised on T-Bone Walker and living the blues. A good cross-section. Pigpen occasionally worked for Troy Weidenheimer at Swan's Music Store. When Troy formed the Zodiacs, who gigged intermittently in 1962 and '63, Pigpen blew harp, Troy was on lead, Garcia sat in on bass, and Bill Kreutzmann handled the drumkit. They were a fundamental seed for the Grateful Dead.

Bluegrass On The Banjo

At this time, Garcia was still mostly playing bluegrass, either with his wife Sarah, who played acoustic to his fiddle or banjo, or with groups like the Hart Valley Drifters [Ken Frankel (mandolin), David Nelson (guitar), Bob Hunter (bass) and Garcia (banjo)], who in 1963 won the amateur bluegrass contest at the Monterey Folk Festival. Eventually they changed their name to Mother Macree's Uptown Jug Champions, and later the Asphalt Jungle Boys. The group, as Garcia remembered, "played any place that would have a jug band, which was almost no place, and that's the reason we finally got into electric stuff . . . it was Pigpen's idea . . . that was his trip . . . and it was just the next step."

Around this time the rock and folk scenes were being blasted apart by two forces which were to have a major cumulative effect on both the potential and enjoyment of rock & roll, and its imagery — the Beatles and Bob Dylan.

To the San Francisco contingent, the reaction to the Beatles was 'Hey, great, that looks like fun'. As Garcia put it, they were "light and having a good time, and they were good too, so it was a combination that was very satisfying on the artistic level . . . they were making people happy. That happy thing — that's the thing that counts — something we could all see right away." On the other hand, "Dylan was able to tell you the truth about the other thing. He was able to talk about the changes you'd go through . . . and say it in a good way, the right way."

By 1964, the jug band had become known as the Warlocks, and when Lesh was persuaded to take up the bass it consisted of Weir (rhythm), Lesh (bass), Garcia (lead), Kreutzmann (drums) and Pigpen as the frontman (vocals, harp and organ). Together they started irregular work around the Bay Area, and against the backdrop of the Free Speech Movement, the Jerry Rubin Movement and the Ramparts Magazine Movement, they soon became incubators of the huge egg that was the next celebration, 'the celebration of truth through fire . . . the ordeal of LSD, before anyone'.

In the late summer of 1964, LSD hit San Francisco like a bomb. With it came a true sense of underground community that centred on Haight-Ashbury — funky, untarnished, no random murders, no heroin, 'the cops didn't even wear bullet-proof vests'.

In this setting two factors grew up together: the kids who were just hanging loose behind acid, wandering round and round the streets bumping into each other; and those like Kesey and Leary, who were involved in professional specifics, in analytical experiments. Naturally, the two were pre-scheduled to meet, and the encounter resulted in the first 'Acid Tests' — a collision-course operated by Kesey's Pranksters and Garcia's good-time pirates, and held together by Bill Graham. The weirdness had begun. The Warlocks became the Grateful Dead — *the Grateful Dead* — the pioneer San Francisco band who played their first gig at Magoo's pizza parlour in June, 1965. At that time the

...utzmann on drums, Phil Lesh on bass and Tom Constanten on keyboards. A line-up that has meant a lot of things to many people.

Robert Ellis

music scene around them was beginning to stabilize: Jefferson Airplane came together, Janis fronted Big Brother and the Holding Company, the Charlatans, Mother Earth and the Sons of Champlin all slowly emerged.

Soon, many of them signed recording deals, and went into the studios. The Dead didn't. They played the bars, the Matrix, the Avalon, the Straight Theatre; long, rambling sets where Pigpen would sing 'In the Midnight Hour' for 40 minutes. Their sound and equipment, masterminded by chemical wizard Stanley Owsley III, was never completely successful, but nonetheless became an embodiment of their fantasies. The stage effect was of a science-fiction tabloid decked out in wild day-glo patterns, emanating the gothic mystery of a horror movie. The band were broke, but they were crazy, free spirits.

And then things changed. In October, 1966, acid was made illegal in California. The Dead were living at 710 Ashbury Street, and at the height of the so-called 'summer of love' they were busted en masse.

By this time the Dead had signed to Warner Brothers, and a three-day recording session in L.A. had produced an album of hyperactive music for the American record market. Despite a mixture of self-penned and standard songs taken at rinky-dink pace with a jangling, over-busy sound, the album sales were minimal and the band was going deeper into debt every day. The machine was running slightly out of control.

By this time Mickey Hart had joined the band as Kreutzmann's mentor. He was a percussionist, not a drummer, and a hypnotist to boot. He actually put Bill the Drummer into a trance while leaping around the stage smashing gongs, cymbals and bells. Mickey's father, Lenny, was a businessman and seeing that the band's financial affairs were crumbling, he offered to become their manager. They accepted. After all, they were making and spending thousands, not tens, of dollars now, and the job was too much for the original managers, Rock Scully and Danny Rifkin. So Lenny Hart took over the accounting.

For the next two years things moved slowly. They spent innumerable hours

Joe Stevens

Centre: Ron 'Pigpen' McKernan. Right:
Jerry Garcia. Above: Bob Weir.

recording, and innumerable weeks mixing down the tapes. 'Anthem Of The Sun' resulted, followed by 'Aoxomoxoa', and finally the culmination of all that the Haight had been and suddenly, was no longer, 'Live Dead'.

Dragon Music

Up to the end of 1969, this was inevitably the strongest side of the band: their onstage warmth and appeal to the street-people, *their* street-people, combined with a stunning, innovative power led mainly by the majesty of Garcia's playing and Weir's chopping rhythm guitar and the thundering, bubbling bass of Phil Lesh. 'Dark Star' from 'Live Dead' will stand for many years as the essence of improvised rock — dragon-music in the extreme, esoteric and asymmetrical.

Meanwhile, the Dead had run up a bill with Warners for about $180,000. Then came Altamont. No one knows why it happened, and despite over-eager critics it wasn't the death of rock, but it certainly had a profound effect on the musicians and old hands of the West Coast. The solution seen by the Grateful Dead and their lyricist Bob Hunter was simply that light is followed by darkness . . . which is again followed by light. 'New Speedway Boogie' is one of Hunter's neatest songs, and captures the effect of the moment perfectly:

'. . . I spent a little time on the mountain,
  spent a little time on the hill
Things went down we don't understand,
  but I think in time we will'

For the Dead, the darkness of those days didn't go so easily. They were busted once more, 'down in New Orleans'. Finally, a showdown with Lenny Hart resulted in him leaving, and old friend John MacIntyre taking over the helm. The Dead had become Uncle John's Band . . . realizing

then that they had been swindled out of large sums of money over the years.

After this, amid financial and legal hassles, the Dead retreated to the studios, and 'Workingman's Dead' became their grip on reality, the only positive action in the midst of huge adversity. The album showed a quieter, more assured band. The sound was light and acoustic, and many of the tracks were recorded live. With its release in the summer of 1970, the Dead reached out to a new audience — and took their old one with them. Suddenly they were national heroes, touring triumphantly with the New Riders Of The Purple Sage, a spin-off band which included John Dawson and Marmaduke from the jug band days, and Spencer Dryden, the earliest and best of the Airplane's drummers. Unnoticed, they even managed a fleeting visit in May, 1970, to play at the Hollywood Festival in England.

Diamond-Faceted

They followed 'Workingman's Dead' with 'American Beauty', firmly establishing Bob Hunter as a writer of strongly melodic songs — direct, terse, and romantic as in 'Attics Of My Mind':

'In the attics of my life, full of cloudy
  dreams unreal
Full of things no tongue can know, and
  lights no eye can see
When there was no ear to hear, you sang
  to me.'

This new material was quickly assimilated into their live act, now diamond-faceted, and it eventually resulted in another 'live' double-set, 'Grateful Dead'. This one was lighter than 'Live Dead'; the band here had a definite spring in its heel — musically they were 'on top'.

Over the next two years, the momentum of this point gave birth to a dozen brain-children: 45 of the family toured Europe at

last, confronting houses full of ecstatic Dead fans every night, bewildering customs officials and hotel chambermaids. During this period, Mickey Hart left, built his own studios, recorded 'Rolling Thunder' and, afterwards, Hunter's first solo effort. Keith Godcheaux also joined on keyboards, adding yet another dimension, and Garcia and Weir had considerable solo successes. The Dead followed their commercial acceptance with a trip back to the roots, and in the summer of 1973 played at Watkin's Glen with the Band and the Allman Brothers to an audience of 600,000 — easily a world record rock crowd. Finally, they broke away from Warners and formed their own company with its own distribution, and subsequently released their first studio album for three years — 'In The Wake Of The Flood'.

The ball was in their court, though the game had now reached astronomical proportions: monthly overheads reached to $100,000; their equipment weighed 23 tons; the basic touring crew was two dozen. Even the quippies (roadies) had a band of their own.

In 1975 the Dead released their 'Blues For Allah' album and then in 1976 a live double album 'Steal Your Face' which consisted of material from concerts at Winterland, San Francisco in 1974.

Music Addict

Garcia, a self-professed music junkie, still found time for other ventures. For a long time he and Merle Saunders were working the Bay Area with John Kahn and Tom Fogerty. Locally known as the Group, together they released three fine albums on Fantasy. Garcia also worked occasionally with organist Howard Wales, with whom he cut 'Hooteroll'; and had a blue-grass group as well — Old And In The Way, who regularly played the bars in Marin County. Never a dull moment for the dedicated guitarist.

And for darkness? By the age of 15 Pigpen was carving out a future in the classic blues mould with a diet of Thunderbird and Ripple. It wasn't a long journey; it reached an inevitable finale. At one point, in 1971, he collapsed with perforated ulcers and a liver full of holes . . . but pulled through. After that he began to play with the band once more, but music and booze were the same thing for Pigpen. The music kept him going but the booze was too much for him and he died not long afterwards. He became just another rock & roll statistic in an ever-lengthening list.

To use Garcia's words again, ''Basically our situation is on the border of collapse all the time''. He is referring to the seed that germinated on Haight-Ashbury, and resulted in the continued struggle for survival in the rock-affected world. Surprisingly, what has grown from that seed has come to realize its earliest, most fundamental and most naïve principles. Those who still adhere to those principles are living on a knife-edge — and enjoying it to the hilt. Once you've mastered it, you just can't forget how to boogie.

STEVE MILLER

Quarter-of-a-million sales on each of his first five albums, a platinum disc for the million-selling 'The Joker' album, the title single of which made no. 1 in the US, and a name as one of the founder figures of the San Francisco acid-rock movement, which changed the face of music in the mid-'60s, were all cast-iron credentials for Steve Miller.

But there was far more to Miller's contribution than that. 'The Gangster Of Love' or 'The Space Cowboy' as he was sometimes known was as important for what he coaxed out of others as for what he did himself.

Like his British counterpart, John Mayall, the transplanted Texan was, through his ever-changing band, a catalyst for a lot that happened on the rock scene.

Boz Scaggs emerged from his band, Miller worked with organist Barry Goldberg and gigged with bluesmen like Muddy Waters, Buddy Guy and Paul Butterfield, and even cut a live album at the Fillmore West with Chuck Berry.

Born in Milwaukee, Wisconsin, the son of a Dallas doctor and raised in the 'Lone Star State', he first recorded (though not commercially) at the age of four-and-a-half and at five was already studying guitar, influenced to no small degree by family friend Les Paul who, besides notching hit records with singing partner Mary Ford,

earned immortality by designing the legendary Les Paul Gibson guitar.

Steve Miller's mother was a singer, an uncle played fiddle in a country band, another was with Paul Whiteman's dance orchestra and he had a younger brother, Jimmy, who was a talented guitarist in the Jeff Beck/Jimi Hendrix mould.

By the age of 12, he was organizing his own band, both music-wise and handling the bookings. Called the Marksmen Combo, the line-up included Boz Scaggs.

He also met local blues hero T-Bone Walker who further developed his interest in black music, and while Miller and Scaggs were both attending the University of Wisconsin in Madison during 1961 they organized a group called the Ardells playing soul and Motown numbers.

Miller's interest in urban blues drew him to Chicago where he spent a couple of years, playing alongside such black greats as Muddy Waters, Buddy Guy and Junior Wells — not just sitting-in, but as a regular member of their bands — and became involved in the growing white Chicago blues scene.

He recalled: "That's why I became mature musically. I wasn't playing with a bunch of kids my own age but with guys of 50."

He met up with Barry Goldberg, who had been organist with Paul Butterfield's band and with the Mike Bloomfield/Buddy Miles band, Electric Flag, and they formed a new group called World War Three. It lasted 10 months but while it was happening musically, managerial troubles led to Miller quitting after their debut single, 'The Mother Song', and two days before work started on a first album for Epic.

Hard-Driving Rock

Two years of hustling, living in slums with little money, and the frustrations he'd experienced with World War Three, sent Miller heading back home where he took a job as a janitor in a Fort Worth recording studio. Part of the deal was that he would get several hours per day of free recording time in exchange for his labours, and it was at this period that he developed many of the ideas which subsequently surfaced in the milestone album, 'Children Of The Future'.

Returning to his studies he went to Europe where he attended the University of Copenhagen, reading comparative literature, history and creative writing. Then, in 1966, he returned to America and moved to San Francisco where he formed the first Steve Miller Blues Band.

With old friends Tim Davis (drums), Curly Cooke (rhythm guitar) and bassist Lonnie Turner and himself on lead guitar, vocals and harmonica, the band produced music which contained elements of the blues but was far more into the hard-driving acid-rock style which was then formulating around San Francisco's Haight-Ashbury district under the aegis of mentor Bill Graham, who put on regular concerts at a decaying dance hall that eventually became Fillmore West.

The first changes occurred six months later when Boz Scaggs caught up with his old pal and replaced Curly Cooke while organist Jim Peterman was added.

Though a leading figure in the emergent San Francisco scene, along with Jefferson Airplane and Grateful Dead, Miller chose to go to England to record his debut album, 'Children Of The Future', feeling that he would get greater artistic freedom there and having enough cash thanks to an advance from Capitol Records following a triumphant appearance at the 1967 Monterey Festival. The album was produced by Glyn Johns, then the hottest person around due to his work as an engineer on the Beatles' 'Sergeant Pepper' album. The combination worked,

the album soon making a dent in the charts.

There were problems though. The band were sharing a mews house in London and Miller left because the dope scene there was getting a bit heavy, but since his clothes were on the premises he got busted with the rest of the band. The newspaper reports got back to his family in Dallas, so he had to rush into a studio with Glyn Johns and record a tape to send to his irate father, explaining everything

that had happened! It all meant that a projected tour had to be cancelled, his debut UK appearance finally coming at the Rainbow in 1972 when he brought an all-new band including black bass player Gerald Johnson whom Miller had discovered backing the Sweet Inspirations on a Presley show.

The follow-up set to 'Children', 'Sailor', released in October 1968, was even better than the first, including the superb

Miller seemed to be finding it increasingly difficult to keep his pulse on what was happening, leading to a run of personnel changes and some below-par recordings with weak material and slap-dash production making him seemingly 'yesterday's man'.

Glyn Johns had produced the first four albums but the pair had then split up, Miller feeling that Johns was trying to control the whole show and was increasingly failing to project Miller's music the way its creator wanted it projected.

'The Joker' put matters right, giving his career its biggest-ever boost and lifting him from being a well-respected rock star with a hard-core following, but whose name was unknown to the great mass public, to being a bona fide pop personality with an American chart-topping single to prove it.

The band had been working hard, playing more than 200 cities in a year and the hit brought an even more demanding round of live appearances so that, after seven or eight years of almost continuous touring, Miller was close to exhaustion.

The solution was a year's lay-off from live performing, starting from May 1974, and ending with his British appearance at the Knebworth Festival in July, 1975.

In the meantime, though, he hadn't been totally inactive, putting down a lot of ideas at the studio in his new home in Nevada and recording with bluesman James Cotton.

Statesman And Superstar

Miller appeared at Knebworth with another new band — Leo Dudek on guitar, Doug Clifford on drums and old cohort Lonnie Turner on bass. He had turned the gig down at first asking, then, with his recording and business schedules complete and the idea of a European holiday appealing, he changed his mind. He appeared as a rather rotund elder statesman of rock, 31 years old and looking well-travelled, but still an amazing personality, a mixture of creative musician, tough businessman and a romantic, happy guy — in short, a real-life rock superstar for the masses.

Way back in 1967, Miller had proved one of the sensations of that year's charismatic Monterey Festival, thanks to a self-designed electronics cabinet which used a graphic equalizer and a tape-loop to produce a variety of sustain and feedback sounds. One reviewer described it as recalling "huge sheets of steel violently shaken."

Knebworth showed that he was still in the forerank of those musicians exploring the wider possibilities of electronic music, without losing touch with the blues.

In 1976 he released 'Fly Like An Eagle' — the result of months of painstaking effort and careful compilation of ideas. Almost three years since the release of 'The Joker' he had produced an equally impressive album which not only captivated his existing followers but also won over a whole new audience of Steve Miller devotees.

'Living In The USA' which became something of a theme for him.

When Scaggs and Peterman left, Miller brought in keyboard men Ben Sidran and Nicky Hopkins (the later a well respected British session-player who had worked on the Rolling Stones' albums and who was to join Quicksilver Messenger Service, another important California-based band). Their work highlighted the highly melodic quality which had come to

Above: The Space Cowboy's guitar technique in action at a US concert. Miller's stage costume contributed to the laid-back bluesman image.

be the band's trademark — the 'Your Saving Grace' and 'Steve Miller Five' albums also being noted for superlative production techniques.

The music scene was beginning to change and with the dawn of the '70s

JANIS JOPLIN

She was a real little earth-mama. A child-woman who sang black country blues gone electric. Her husky voice rasped out the notes and people said she was the greatest white female blues singer ever, and they always qualified it like that — 'white and female'.

Maybe, if she had lasted a few years more, Janis could have made it all the way to becoming *the* 'greatest blues singer'. Still, she *was* a legend in her own time. She zapped in at the end of the twin-set, pearls and brogues era — when girl singers were either wholesome and happy, or chirpily sexy — and showed that being a girl didn't automatically put you into one of those moulds . . . in fact, she showed you could be a girl *and* have soul.

Janis Joplin was an anachronism in her small hometown of Port Arthur in Texas. She was a beatnik weirdo who didn't fit into the routine of small-town life at all. Born there on January 19th, 1943, by the time she was 14, the locals — with their middle-class values and middle-income habits — had decided she was some kind of revolutionary. At high school she dressed differently and cared about different things, and as a result had few friends that she could relate to. At this stage though, neither she nor her family — younger brother Michael and younger sister Laura — had any great musical leanings, but, according to her father, she read, she painted and she thought.

By all accounts her teenage years were typical of the '50s — boring, stifling and endless. So, although it's difficult to believe, as a teenager Janis was quiet, introspective, lonely . . . and waiting.

Texas isn't the place for outrageous people, and as Janis said, ''they laughed me out of class, out of town and out of the state''.

She also had to bear with the musical mish-mash of the '50s — the untainted petting of the high school jingles, those shallow old tunes that came floating out of every transistor in town, with no meaning, no guts, no bottom. She was 17 before she discovered the blues, in the form of Leadbelly and Bessie Smith, and for the next few years Bessie Smith was her idol. She played her music endlessly, and naturally she sang her songs . . . in an incredible blues moan that was light years away from anything that was happening musically in Texas at that time. Years later, when Janis spoke of Bessie Smith, she said, ''she showed me the air and taught me how to fill it. She's the reason I started singing really''. (Janis' feelings for this blues queen were so strong that she even organised a headstone for her grave.)

Free Beer And Hillbillies

When Janis finished high school, she began singing whenever she got the opportunity. Locally, she began to gain a reputation as a blues singer, mostly singing in a little bar outside of Austin, Texas. It was a Saturday night place, with bring-your-own guitars, free beer and real live hillbillies. Still, she hadn't yet escaped the conformity of her upbringing, and so enrolled at a college to study to be a teacher — giving up the coffee-bar circuit where she had been singing.

College life, however, was no more appetising than that of high school, and so when Chet Helms, an old friend of hers, appeared on the scene, she decided to drop out of college and head for San Francisco with him. She was only 18, and California was a whole new world. She stayed around there for five years, singing in the bars and folk clubs, playing auto-harp, and becoming a high-flying speed freak who didn't have too much going for her. But she *was* learning to be free, and no longer felt a monster in a world of goody-goods.

Then, in the mid-'60s, the 'underground' started to really happen strongly in California. The beards and hair flowed unshaped and untamed. The clothes were long, wild and spacey. They were improvised, colourful and precious. They were timeless in their non-adherence to a fashion format. The young lived in a charming mix-up of squalor and beauty — brown rice and black beans, chenille curtains, embroidered cushions, Spanish pots and Tibetan prints, broken toilets and bead curtains, blocked-up refrigerators, flax matting and scrubbed wooden tables. Wax-eyed friends flowed in and out, sipped camomile tea, and carried enamelled snuff boxes that belied the sagging ceilings above them. And in all this, Janis sowed her oats without a break, and in a spate of burnt-out tiredness, decided to return home and give the straight life one more chance.

She sang the blues in her rawest, most sensuous fashion, letting her tearaway voice out at full-throttle. This satin-shine, this tender tart, made them get up and move.

This was 1965, and it was the year that San Francisco finally came together, musically. Underground clubs started up, including the now legendary Fillmore Auditorium. The psychedelic rockers and the acid rockers came in the shape of Jefferson Airplane, the Grateful Dead, Captain Beefheart, the Doors, Moby Grape, Country Joe and the Fish, the Fugs and Velvet Underground. They were mostly community bands, friends who just happened to come together and play for fun. They were communal and tolerant, and they were rebelling against materialistic and bigoted repression — it was love versus violence.

The mid-'60s were a time of acid art, light shows — vibrating, merging splodges of colour that blended silkily and serenely, glowing milkily-pearlescent and translucent across the walls. And their music reflected this in intense details. Janis' Texan friend Chet Helms, who was organising the first hippie dances at the Avalon Ballroom (where Big Brother and the Holding Company eventually established themselves) became their manager. At the time, though, they needed another singer, and Chet persuaded them that Janis was the right one.

He drove to Texas to see her, and Janis threw in college for the final time. Janis and Big Brother — Sam Andrew and Jim Gurley on guitars, Peter Albin on bass and Dave Getz on drums — regularly worked the Avalon and other small gigs around the Bay. Janis learned to fuse her blues with the strength of Big Brother's powerful amplifiers. She discovered that the only way to cope with an electric rock band was to explode. She sang wild and free. She screamed into that high-energy rock music, and the hippies couldn't get enough of her. Big Brother were fast moving into the top group ratings, along with the Grateful Dead and Jefferson Airplane. Janis was living with Country Joe at the time, and when their relationship ended he wrote a song about her, called 'Janis' in his album 'Fixin' To Die'.

She was singing wilder and louder than ever and her voice hid her youth. It was gravelly and gutsy, and it hollered, screeched and seduced everyone with its raw caresses. It didn't take long before Big Brother got an offer to record, from a small Chicago outfit called Mainstream. It was a disastrous liason, and the album 'Big Brother And The Holding Company' wasn't released until after the Monterey Pop Festival, when the record company were absolutely certain that they would make a killing with it. Big Brother tried to prevent its release, as they had improved immensely in the interval, but the album nevertheless sold fantastically (this was still at a time when Janis was *in* the band, rather than *being* the band).

Monterey Pop

Big Brother continued to gig and rehearse three or four times a week, and Janis was by now ripping into the blues with a blown-out, earthy passion. The Monterey Pop Festival of June '67 was the big break for Janis and Big Brother, and after months of practising in the Haight, they were ready for it, and so were 50,000 love-freaks. It was their first real festival, and they turned on to the magic brew of love, flowers and music. From Otis Redding to Ravi Shankar the music was amazing, but no one had any expectations of Big Brother, who were relatively unknown outside San Francisco. They had to follow on from the Who and Hendrix . . . and they made it.

Janis' rendering of 'Big Mama' and 'Ball And Chain' broke the place apart, and they couldn't get enough of her. It all came out front – her tough, hooker voice tore at their insides. She was a mean blues singer with sex flowing out to the audience in a hot, full rush. It was crude and rough and tremendously important. Janis was the big discovery of the festival and the rock critics couldn't write enough about her. Her pure animal grace as she moved and stomped – letting her tearaway voice out at full-throttle – whipped her audience again and again into a frenzy of applause.

Big Brother had arrived, and Janis had made the transition from a street-singer to a rock star. By January '68, they had signed with Albert Grossman – then managing Bob Dylan – and were ready to start touring. By the end of August, their tours had included the Fillmore East and the Newport Folk Festival, and Janis had become a true, husky-voiced earth-mama yelling her aching hurt. She said, 'she'd rather not sing than sing quiet', and she flooded her fans with her deep anguish. Her whisky-soaked, Southern Comfort voice could touch on a tender quietness too, but it was her wailing and whoring moaning that plugged the audience into her.

Janis controlled the entire audience with her body. She tore right into them, with her breasts and hair and beads flying, her clothes the ultimate in extravagance:

*'Are your clothes matching your soul?
Your soul goes through changes, you're
always feeling all things at once. So why
not wear all things at once – its groovy,
its real.'*

Her spaced-out clothes amazed and delighted every male in the audience. She dripped feathers and bangles as her impassioned voice blasted the lids off their minds. Her satin and silk slipped tight over her heaving breasts as she groaned into the cold steel microphone.

In her no-faking, tender-tart clothes, she whipped herself into a lather of frenzied singing and boogying. It was a huge and raw performance, and gradually the band fell further and further behind her. However, when 'Cheap Thrills' came out in September '68, it earned a Gold Record almost immediately. The band had a full rock sound and Janis came across as a powerful, confident singer. Some of the best tracks were 'Summertime', 'Piece Of My Heart' and 'Turtle Blues', written by Janis herself:

*'I once had a daddy,
He said he'd give me everything in sight.
So I said, honey, I want the sunshine,
   yeah,
An' take the stars out of the night.'*

Soon after the success of 'Cheap Thrills', Janis and Big Brother split up. Their final concert together was appropriately enough with Chet Helms' Family Dogg. Janis antagonised a lot of her fans with the split, but there were too many tensions for the band to be able to hold together any longer.

She had difficulty choosing a new band, telling a good sax from a faker. She was doing a mammoth task, virtually carrying the whole band by herself. She wanted a thicker sound – a soul sound – and the final line-up was Sam Andrew (from Big Brother), lead guitar; Bill King, organ; Marcus Doubleday, trumpet; Terry Clements on alto sax (both formerly of the Electric Flag and Buddy Miles Express); Brad Campbell, bass; and Ron Markowitz, drums. She toured with them until December '69, and although they never bombed out completely, they were never much more than a back-up band, and somehow never quite captured the magic of Big Brother. They had recorded an album called 'Kozmic Blues', which was released in November '69 and received very mixed reviews, although it was generally agreed that 'Work Me Lord', 'Try' and 'One Good Man', had all the tough, appealing essence of Janis in them. But for all that, her voice had not heightened its magic, and critics began to ask her if her voice was going. With her usual below-the-belt bounce, she replied: "People like their blues singers dying; they don't like them rocking – I'm rocking, at least I think I am."

She was right, she was first and foremost a blues singer, and there is a tradition attached to that tag, one of 'hardship, tragedy and early death'. Janis' answer to that was: "Just have a good time. I juice up real good and that's what I have. Man, I'd rather have 10 years of superhypermost, than live to be 70 by sitting in some goddam chair watching TV. Right now is where you are, how can you wait?"

Full-Tilt Boogie Band

In mid-April, 1970, Janis re-appeared with Big Brother and the Holding Company (plus Nick Gravenites) at the Fillmore West. They played all their old numbers and everyone loved them. But everything really came together for Janis in May, when she formed her Full-Tilt Boogie Band. The five-piece band included John Till, lead guitar; Brad Campbell, bass; Richard Bell, piano; Ken Pearson, organ and Clark Pierson, drummer.

The group was on the same wavelength as Janis, and the effect was five really good musicians making a tight sound and playing as if they'd been together for years. Their first official gig was on June 12th 1970, at Freedom Hall in Louisville, and it was wilder and more magical than anything that had ever happened for Janis before. She sang the blues in her rawest, most jean-creaming fashion, and everyone rocked in their seats as her high energy poured over them in endless waves. Her voice blew the walls apart and this tender tart made them get up and move. She was a sensuous satin-shine, who would sing until she dropped.

By September, they had almost finished recording their album, with Paul Rothchild as producer. It included two tracks written by Janis, 'Mercedes Benz' and 'Move Over', Kris Kristofferson's memorable 'Me And Bobby McGee', and one that said everything there was to say about Janis, 'Get It While You Can'. They were mostly slower numbers than before, and when the album was posthumously released as 'Pearl', it played like a tribute to a great lady who had been buried alive in the blues.

Dual Deaths

She died on October 3rd, 1970, after accidentally injecting an overdose of heroin into her arm. Another death had been added to the toll of artists who had been at Monterey – Otis Redding, Brian Jones, Al Wilson, Hendrix and then Janis. Hendrix had died only three weeks before, and the similarity in both their lives and deaths was uncanny. They were both 27, and had both made it big at Monterey. They both poured out solid sexuality on the stage, and were both preparing new songs with new bands to reinstate themselves as rock stars. Lastly, they both neutralised their lives with narcotics.

It seemed as though no one ever realised how lonely and insecure Janis was, or how much she depended on drugs. Yet she gave them a clue when she said, "I'm going to write a song about making love to 25,000 people in a concert and then going back to my room alone." Her world was up onstage, and that was a reality that could only extend to a couple of hours a day. It was her high, her Nirvana, her pinnacle of pleasure. How then could the rest of the day match up? The surreal world of plastic planes, shiny-tiled motels, coffin-sized concrete dressing-rooms and pre-packaged food was too hard to take. It was inevitable that Southern Comfort would not always be enough. As Deborah Landau in her book *Janis Joplin – Her Life And Times* said:

'What more lonely way to die, than alone
in a motel room in Los Angeles, feeling
great and being that careless, blowing
the whole thing, all alone, quietly before
she was ready.'

CREEDENCE CLEARWATER REVIVAL

Creedence Clearwater Revival were always something of an anachronism, a throwback, a band out of their real time. Coming to prominence in 1968, in an era of psychedelic, underground and increasingly complex 'progressive' rock, Creedence chose to base their own style very firmly and very obviously in the simple, direct and immediately accessible rock & roll of the mid-1950s.

In an era when in the wake of the Beatles' 'Sgt. Pepper' the *album* was widely held to be the only truly worthwhile rock commodity, Creedence embarked upon a string of classic hit *singles*. And in an era when most bands changed personnel nearly as often as they changed their socks, the members of Creedence had stuck together for almost 10 years before their first real breakthrough to national success.

But though old-fashioned and in many ways unfashionable, Creedence were also an enormously popular band, by a long way

the most commercially successful white American act of their day: Gold Album followed Gold Single, and both followed sold-out tours apparently inexorably, until their final break-up in October 1972.

Creedence were a band out of time, who demonstrated that the times were to some degree out of joint. Then, despite psychedelia and drug-rock and the growth of a real or imagined counter-culture, Creedence made it clear that there were still millions of kids looking for the kind of music they could play on juke-boxes, cruise to on car radios, dance to at parties. That there was still a huge demand for fairly simple and straightforward rock & roll.

Unchallenged Mainstream Band

Creedence filled that demand, and were able to occupy the mainstream of American rock almost unchallenged for the better part of five years. Moreover, they were able to use their authority as a definitive mainstream band to promote ideas and attitudes some way outside the general rock mainstream.

Officially, Creedence Clearwater Revival came into existence on the first day of

1968. Before that, a long way before that, there were the Blue Velvets: Doug Clifford, Stu Cook and John Fogerty. Three 13-year-olds who got together in 1959 at El Cerrito High School in the then quiet (pre-Free Speech Movement) north Californian suburb of Berkeley, near San Francisco. It was John Fogerty's idea:
''. . . one day I was listening to the Corvettes on the radio and boom! . . . I said to myself 'Gee, I could have thought of that name. Corvettes. Like the car . . . And gee, I could make a record like that.'''

The Blue Velvets played at the local school hops, often joined by John's elder brother Tom. Then Tom would sing lead and they would be billed as Tom Fogerty and the Blue Velvets. All four kids were Berkeley born and bred, middle-class and middle income, playing and imitating the music of poor white southerners and northern city ghetto blacks.

In 1964, the Blue Velvets moved up to semi-professional status, acquiring a recording contract with a local San Francisco label, Fantasy. Despite the group's strong objections, Fantasy insisted on a change of name. And so, in the wake of Beatlemania and the British Invasion —

a devastating experience for the native American recording industry – the Blue Velvets became the Golliwogs. It was under this unlikely name that they released a string of mostly unsuccessful singles between 1965 and 1967, all of them now long deleted and unavailable.

Music was still a hobby rather than a full-time occupation. The Golliwogs played primarily in bars in and around the Berkeley area, working very hard and to little appreciation. A very character-building experience, as John Fogerty would recall later in 'Lodi':

*'If I only had a dollar, for every song I've
  sung
And every time I've had to play while
  people sat there drunk
You know I'd catch the next train back to
  where I live
Oh Lord, I'm stuck in Lodi again.'*

During this period, the Golliwogs scored just one moderate-size regional hit single, 'Brown-Eyed Girl'. John Fogerty was now singing lead and Tom had stepped back, confining himself to rhythm guitar: "I could sing, but he had a *sound*." With Doug Clifford on drums and Stu Cook on bass, the line-up of the future Creedence was already fixed. And John Fogerty, lead singer, lead guitarist and soon to be the band's one and only songwriter, was now undisputed leader. If this caused any conflict between the brothers back then, it took a very long time to break the surface.

The Golliwogs Turn Professional

In 1967, control of the Fantasy label passed to one Saul Zaentz, a man with more imagination and more faith in the band. And so, after nearly 10 years without real success, the band decided on one last all-out effort to break through. They turned professional, devoted all their time to music, chose a new name, and made one more new start.

Myths cluster around that new name. The usual story is: they had a friend called Creedence, they saw a TV beer commercial about clear water, they knew there had to be a revival. Creedence Clearwater Revival. Anyway, it was a great name, and it somehow exactly represented the music upon which they would build their new career.

Under the nominal guidance of Saul Zaentz, Creedence went into the studio and cut a first album, titled simply 'Creedence Clearwater Revival'. That album, with its stereotyped Ralph J. Gleason, 'San Francisco Explosion' sleevenotes, undoubtedly profited from the then widespread interest in West Coast music. And yet, the music inside the sleeve actually bore very little relationship to the so-called 'San Francisco Sound'. It was mostly very tough, hard-edged rock & roll and blues, with a clean and relatively uncluttered production that often seemed to hark back to the two-track Memphis sound of Sam Phillips' old Sun studio rock & roll classics.

The usual San Francisco album of the period (Country Joe and the Fish, the Jefferson Airplane, the Grateful Dead, and so on) was cool, spacey and very cerebral, featuring lengthy and complex instrumental passages, much apparently directionless riffing, and lyrics concerning drugs, religious insights and universal love. The Creedence sound, and in particular Fogerty's singing, was hot, raucous and urgent. The songs were tightly arranged and performed, the instrumental passages kept neat and concise: only one track, the old Dale Hawkins rock & roll standard 'Susie Q', broke the five-minute barrier. The lyrics referred only to universal rock & roll and blues mythology: women, love, sex, poverty, misery. This was music that knew exactly where it was going. It was, predominantly, music to excite the body rather than the mind.

Standard R & R Numbers

Though John Fogerty had written five original songs for that album, it was the two rock & roll standards – 'Susie Q' and the old Screaming Jay Hawkins number 'I Put A Spell On You' – that stood out as the strongest cuts. Both were released, simultaneously, as singles, and both reached the US Top 10.

So Creedence began with an unusual name and a distinctly unusual image: that of a rock & roll revival band. Their next single, 'Proud Mary' – first in a long sequence of contemporary rock & roll classics written by John Fogerty – redefined and extended that image:

*'Cleaned a lot of plates in Memphis
Pumped a lot of gas down in New Orleans
But I never saw the good side of the city
'Til I hitched a ride on a riverboat queen
Big wheel keeps on turning
Proud Mary keeps on burning
Rolling, rolling on the river . . .*

Raised and based in Berkeley, John Fogerty now led his band into a celebration of the mythology of the American South-West, producing something which the critics would immediately tag 'swamp rock'. Their second album, from which 'Proud Mary' was culled, was called 'Bayou Country', and included one song which advanced the claim to be 'Born On The Bayou'. Their third album was entitled 'Green River', and featured a cover photograph of the band apparently deep in that bayou country: the photograph was taken in Berkeley's Tilden Park.

Since John Fogerty was by now taking sole production credits for these albums, and writing nearly all the songs, one must assume that he was largely responsible for this exercise in image-building. And it was, indeed, a curious image for a north Californian band to adopt. But when Creedence sang those songs, they were somehow entirely convincing. John Fogerty managed to translate his obsession with the Old West – with a land of freedom and open spaces, where the catfish bite, the bootleg stills bubble, and barefoot girls

Chris Walter

From left to right: Doug Clifford, Tom

dance in the moonlight – into compelling and authoritative music. For the city dwellers who largely made up Creedence's audience, these songs brought alive what was to them a dead and gone American landscape.

Co-existing with these swamp rock archetypes, a secondary theme begins to appear in Fogerty's songs, from the 'Green River' album on. Moving from a celebration of freedom in the American past, Fogerty arrived at a deeply pessimistic view of the American present. Creedence's big hit single of mid-1969, 'Bad Moon Rising', was a furiously energetic cry of despair: 'I hear the voice of rage and ruin', Fogerty rants like some Biblical prophet, 'One eye is taken for an eye'. The 'nasty weather' here, though outside of human control, isn't just some arbitrary whim of fate: it's very clearly seen as a punishment, something that we've brought upon ourselves.

Very cautiously at first, Creedence were beginning to use their authority as a mainstream good-time rock & roll band to put over messages distinct from the usual rock mainstream. These messages were, loosely speaking, 'political'. Not defiantly political, like the songs of the Jefferson Airplane of that period, nor obnoxiously

Fogerty, Stu Cook and John Fogerty.

political, like the later John Lennon; but political all the same, in the sense that *any* comment about the way people live is political.

Another song on the 'Green River' album, 'Wrote A Song For Everyone', made the scope of John Fogerty's political vision a lot more clear. The song starts out as an apparent recollection of his short and disastrous enlistment in the US Army in 1967: 'Saw myself a goin'/Down to war in June'. Of that experience, Fogerty has recalled: "I had to convince myself I was a slave." The song then dives into apparent myth . . . 'Richmond's 'bout to blow up, communications failed'. Is that history, Civil War vintage? Is it a headline from yesterday's newspaper? Or is it a glimpse into the future?

'. . . If you see the answer, now's the time
    to say
All I want, all I want, is to get you down
    and pray'

Pray. Fogerty's Catholic upbringing continually breaks through into these political tracts, turning them into morality tales:

'. . . Saw the people standing, thousand
    years in chains

Somebody says, it's different now, look
    it's just the same

The music is as slow and turgid as 'Bad Moon Rising' is fast and urgent, and it creates a powerful mood of despair.

. . . Wrote a song for everyone, wrote a
    song for truth
Wrote a song for everyone, and I couldn't
    even talk to you'.

At no stage in their career did Creedence become a fully-fledged political-rock band. They played benefits when the cause seemed right, they gave financial support to the Indian occupation of Alcatraz, but they still made a great deal of money for themselves and were primarily a commercial rock & roll band. Essentially, Creedence were a band with a certain integrity. They tried to make music that was true to what they themselves believed, they tried to respond honestly to the needs of their audience. They tried, also, not to bore their audience to tears. Political songs were just one strand in their music, but an important and necessary strand. And Creedence would make some of the most moving and dignified political songs in the history of rock.

At most, in these songs, Creedence stood out against man's inhumanity to man, and for individual freedom. They stood for the kind of freedom that Fogerty glimpsed in the American past, for the kind of freedom that they found in rock & roll. In a period when American police and state agencies appeared to be doing their best to repeal the Bill of Rights, that was enough to make Creedence a dangerously revolutionary outfit.

Urban Landscape

With their fourth album, 'Willy And The Poorboys', Creedence largely abandoned swamp rock for a more urban landscape. The cover photograph has them playing skiffle-style out on the ghetto streets, playing for the poor black kids. The album itself kicks off with 'Down On The Corner', a tribute to street-corner rock & roll. It also contains several more 'political' songs: 'Fortunate Son' about the folks born with silver spoons and star-spangled eyes who send you off to fight their wars; 'Don't Look Now', about the real roots of middle-class affluence. But on the whole it was a much brighter and more optimistic album, and — many people thought — perhaps their most consistent to date.

Finally, though, Creedence music had developed around an ideological inconsistency that John Fogerty could never properly resolve. On the one hand, Creedence were a commercial rock & roll band, celebrating the social and emotional liberation that a whole generation of Americans had gained from rock & roll. But on the other hand, they were well aware of — and anxious to comment on — the desperate social/political situation in which that music was flourishing.

Balancing between these two obsessions, Creedence drifted into a kind of schizophrenia. In early 1970, for example, they chose to issue two songs from their fifth album, 'Cosmo's Factory', as a double-sided single: 'Travellin' Band'/'Who'll Stop The Rain?' Both songs subsequently became US hits. Together, they made very clear the Creedence contradiction.

Golden Days Of Rock

'Travellin' Band' was simple enough — about a rock & roll band on the road and set to the tune of Little Richard's 'Good Golly Miss Molly'. It recalled those simple golden days when all a rock & roller had to worry about was getting to his next gig on time. The other side of the single, 'Who'll Stop The Rain?' — perhaps John Fogerty's best song ever — was a slow and deeply textured allegory:

'Long as I remember, the rain been coming
    down . . . .
Clouds of mystery pouring confusion on the
    ground'

Once again, bad weather fills in for the forces of destruction and decay. The second verse apparently recalls the biblical myth of the Tower of Babel. Corporate man has created an edifice to displease the gods:

'I went down to Virginia, seeking shelter
    from the storm
Caught up in the fable, I watched the tower
    grow
Five year plans and new deals, wrapped
    in golden chains
And I wonder, still I wonder
Who'll stop the rain'

What was it, Fogerty seemed to be asking, that made rock & roll necessary? It was technology, bureaucracy, voluntary slavery, Five Year Plans and New Deals. Rock & roll was an escape from those golden chains, but — as the final verse points out — actually only a very frail and fragile substitute for real freedom and dignity and community. At best, a reminder of things lost:

'Heard the singers playing, how we cheered
    for more
The crowd had rushed together, trying to
    keep warm
Still the rain kept falling, falling on my ears
And I wonder, still I wonder,
Who'll stop the rain?'

The song was written after Woodstock, and enjoyed success after the Rolling Stones' catastrophic concert at Altamont. But its terms of reference are rather wider than that. Yet 'Who'll Stop The Rain?' has finally very little significance in the Creedence canon. It was just the hit record that came after 'Travellin' Band' and before 'Up Around The Bend' (a further celebration of the joys of rock & roll and the open country). On the 'Cosmo's Factory' album it's sandwiched between a redundant recapitulation of the early Elvis hit, 'My Baby Left Me', and an admittedly spectacular work-out on 'I Heard It Through The Grapevine'.

Undisputed leader of Creedence Clearwater, John Fogerty, plays lead guitar. Insert: Stu on bass and Doug on drums.

Finally, Creedence were just a little too shy about their political commitments, with the result that no one ever took the band particularly seriously in their political role. For every 'Who'll Stop The Rain?' there were two songs like 'Travellin' Band', affirming that everything was going to be alright if we kept on rocking.

The four-man Creedence made just one more album, 'Pendulum', released in 1971. A very stiff and processed-sounding album, with lots of overdubbed instruments and some good but by now over-familiar tunes. It seemed that John Fogerty was finally running out of ideas.

Creedence had scored no less than three double-sided hit singles from 'Cosmo's Factory'. They were the top-selling album artists of 1970 in the States, ahead of even the Beatles. Everything they touched seemed to turn to gold. And yet, remorseless tensions were building up inside the group. Resentment at John Fogerty's star role, long-suppressed rivalry between the older and younger brother. Something had to give. Tom Fogerty walked out.

'Creedence Clearwater Revival', Doug Clifford once affirmed, 'was definitely a fifth person outside of the four of us. The whole is bigger than any individual. Like a marriage . . .' The marriage had not yet broken down irretrievably, but it continued on very different terms. The three-man Creedence agreed to 'democratise' the band. Doug Clifford and Stu Cook were now to take an equal share of the responsibility for running the band, and assume an equal share of the songwriting and production duties. As for Tom Fogerty, he was happy to be out of it and going his own way.

A successful Creedence tour of Europe followed. But when they went into the studios to cut what would turn out to be the very last Creedence album, 'Mardi Gras', released in early 1972, the weakness of the new arrangement showed through. After nearly 15 years in the back line, Doug Clifford and Stu Cook had earned the right to try and sing their own songs. But when it came down to it, they appeared to be incapable of distinguishing between what was good and what was bad in their productions. The new democratic arrangement seemed to imply a complete absence of self-criticism or selectivity.

For every good song Cook or Clifford wrote, there seemed to be a total atrocity waiting to cancel it out. And meanwhile John Fogerty confined himself to just new songs, only one of which had any real substance: 'Someday Never Comes', the group's very last hit.

'Mardi Gras' took a pounding from the critical establishment. Jon Landau, elder statesman of rock, led the way in *Rolling Stone*, dismissing it as 'the worst album I have ever heard from a major rock band'. John Fogerty, he implied, was a genius entrapped by vicious mediocrity.

At any rate, the generally poor reception of 'Mardi Gras' meant the end of Creedence Clearwater Revival: they announced their decision to call it quits on October 16th, 1972. Doug Clifford made a solo album. John Fogerty formed the Blue Ridge Rangers, featuring himself on guitars, steel drums, fiddle, voices and everything else, and made an album of country standards. And then Tom Fogerty, Stu Cook and Doug Clifford teamed up yet again to make an album, 'Joyful Resurrection'.

We don't know, yet, the effect of all this on John Fogerty's music. Blue Ridge Rangers was an interesting project, but John Fogerty was always a better songwriter than arranger, singer or musician. Until we hear enough of his own new songs, we won't know what, if anything, he might have lost in the wreckage of Creedence. There were four individuals in Creedence Clearwater Revival, not just one. We may never hear their like again, for Creedence were something special.